Portrait of Geoffrey Jellicoe by Michael Tree, 1990

Gardens
of the
Mind

The Genius of
Geoffrey Jellicoe

Michael Spens

Antique Collectors' Club

ISBN 1 85149 088 4

Published for the Antique Collectors' Club
by the Antique Collectors' Club Ltd

British Library CIP Data
    Gardens of the mind: the genius of Geoffrey Jellicoe
    712.60941

Printed in England by the Antique Collectors' Club Ltd, Woodbridge, Suffolk

CONTENTS

Colour Illustrations and Drawings

Some years ago the editor of *Studio International,* Michael Spens, called at my flat to discuss a possible article on my work. Later he called again to show me the proposed illustrations, staying with something else obviously on his mind. Soon afterwards he asked if he could write this study. Of course I agreed. In due time I travelled north to his remote home in Fife where, with his wife Janet and two eloquent little girls to assist, we discussed progress.

Initially we visited together Rustington in Sussex, where I had spent much of my childhood between classical sea and romantic downs. He follows me through my early schools, both set in impressionable landscapes, and thence to the Architectural Association School, where in 1925 I began my professional career with the publication of *Italian Gardens of the Renaissance.* From this important beginning he follows me on through my works to the present day. As a distinguished architect and a discerning critic of the arts in general, he is well equipped to penetrate my work and its underlying meaning, and to reveal and discuss the first ever recognisable attempts to harness the subconscious to the cause of visible landscape design.

Geoffrey Jellicoe

Highpoint 1991

ACKNOWLEDGEMENTS

This book would not have materialised without the encouragement and enthusiasm for the subject of John Steel. More than exceptional, this ran to contributing his own photographs of Italian gardens, and to invaluable advice on the structure of the book. I am also most grateful both to Diana Steel, and to Cherry Lewis who edited with great skill.

Particular gratitude is also due to Mr Michael and Lady Anne Tree for allowing me to get to know and understand Shute through several visits; to Lord and Lady Pym for their hospitality at Everton; to Mr and Mrs Simon Bowes-Lyon for introducing me to St Pauls Walden Bury at length; to Mr Peter Atkins for instilling in me the secrets of Galveston and the Moody Foundation; to Roger Mayne the photographer and his wife Ann Jellicoe the playwright for, in Lady Jellicoe's sad absence, letting me into the family fold of close Jellicoes with tolerance and generosity. I would also like to thank Miss Jane Flavell of The Vinery, Rustington, Sussex, for the bonus of an afternoon's visit there with Sir Geoffrey.

Lord and Lady Esher, personal friends of Geoffrey Jellicoe, helped me understand his long career, its trials, tribulations and great successes. As Lionel Brett, Lord Esher is a past President of the R I B A and a former Rector of the Royal College of Art. A successful architect, at one time in association with Geoffrey Jellicoe, he is also author of numerous books, the latest *The Glory of the English House,* and therefore ideally qualified to write the Foreword to this book, for which I am most grateful.

I also acknowledge a debt to Roger Last of BBC's *Omnibus* who both publicised the book's title by adopting it for his superb film coverage of Sir Geoffrey's work, and shared numerous and invaluable discussions about individual gardens and landscapes with me.

To Dawn Waddell, University of St Andrews, thanks are due for her invaluable typing skill; also to Jamie Gardiner-Hill, for his photographs specially commissioned for the chapter on Shute House.

Special thanks are also due to the organisers of the 1988 Boston Conference of the International Federation of Landscape Architects, the American Society of Landscape Architects, for their generosity in inviting me and their hospitality there. An A S L A standing ovation has to be seen to be believed; then too one could see the global warmth of feeling and esteem for the subject, their former president and co-founder.

Finally, my deepest gratitude must go to Sir Geoffrey Jellicoe himself, who has transformed the author's task from what can be an infinitely regressive maze, into an open landscape of discovery.

FOREWORD

Having known Geoffrey Jellicoe for many years, and for some of them shared with his firm the corner house in Queen Anne's Gate which was once Lutyens' office, I write of him with great affection. His round face and figure, his ever optimistic nature and his lovely combination of unpretentiousness, underlying seriousness and sense of fun, have ensured this anyway. He seems to have the secret not merely of survival but of eternal youth.

He grew up just in time for the fun years of the 1920s but was unlucky, like all creative people of his generation, in living the whole central section of his working life through economic depression, world war and post-war austerity, and then being out of sympathy with the brutalism of the precarious boom/bust society of the Wilson era. Fortunately his splendid vitality preserved him for the 1980s, when all over the world people and planners were inclined to give up on the problems of the great cities and to turn to the threatened landscape, the so-called 'Natural World', in a passionate determination to understand its roots in time, to safeguard it as our ultimate resource and to enhance it by intelligent intervention. It was then that his lifetime study of the philosophy of landscape design from the Far East to Western Europe and of its reflection in art from the Renaissance to Surrealism and abstraction brought him back into close contact with the concerns of the young.

This book is a comprehensive and sympathetic study of his landscape work over most of our century, and is graced by his own soft, sensitive, so English design drawings. His major works, as is the nature of landscapes and gardens, have been developed over decades and some will only mature in the next century. Change, he believes, is of the essence, yet obviously must somehow be controlled. This is one of the many questions the book will raise in the reader's mind. Our own famous landscapes of the Augustan Age, now in decay after their Victorian climax, were only achieved because they were in the single ownership of very rich men. Now even the very rich can only make gardens, not landscapes, so that Vignola's open-air ballrooms become more relevant than the broad brush of Capability Brown. Nor have public authorities in the western world the slightest chance or wish to take their place. Just when our environmental concerns stretch to the horizon, indeed worldwide, the designer is back in the medieval world of the paradise garden, the garden for privileged, solitary contemplation. Elsewhere over the landscape at large, money and materialism seem to rule all.

Geoffrey Jellicoe's thought, and much of his writing, has been concerned with this problem of bringing together the new interest in pre-history, in myth and symbolism, in the psychology of art, and our enormous power over the landscape. In 1975, summing up his and his wife's magisterial *The Landscape of Man* he asked:

'Now that we know and can assess the forces battering our planet, can they first be resisted by the defensive mechanism of instinct and then controlled and put to work by the intellect?'

The question remains unanswered — probably unanswerable. Shelley, too, had hopes that the poets might save mankind. But what outlived him were not his large ideas but the works of his lyrical genius.

Lionel Esher

PROLOGUE TO A JOURNEY

'Architecture is in deep trouble, whereas landscape architecture thrives'

'Landscape design will transcend architecture as the mother of the arts'

July 1988. Crammed up against the central tourist class bulkhead of the TWA flight, Geoffrey Jellicoe consoled fellow passenger Sylvia Crowe with the exhortation: 'We must remember we are going as pilgrims and this is a pilgrimage'. It seemed to me that this might well be a paradigm for the whole course of Jellicoe's life, and the protracted if inspired journey it has been.

On arrival in Boston, he was delivered safely by a capacious air-conditioned limousine to the Conference of the International Federation of Landscape Architects, as hosted by the American Society, a worthy destination indeed.

Jellicoe, in his keynote address to the assembled delegates, reminded them of the simple origins of their organisation in which he had played a formative role; of early conferences composed of a few enthusiasts, from Cambridge in 1948 to Vienna in 1954; of boat trips, of open-air meals. Very shortly, however, he turned to the future. Now his quoted sources ranged from Dubuffet, to Taoism, to Buddhism, to C H Waddington, geneticist and writer on art, to Juhani Pallasmaa, contemporary architectural theorist.

The message was: 'Architecture is in deep trouble, whereas landscape architecture thrives'. Jellicoe went on to claim that 'in due time, perhaps even in the next forty years, landscape design will transcend architecture as the mother of the arts'. And he wound up: 'Beauty [is] the ultimate goal of our federation and its supreme contribution to peace on earth'. Jellicoe's closing exhortation to every individual, student or frustrated practitioner, was to make and keep 'intimate contact with some fragment of the sister arts of music, sculpture or painting'. To a four minute standing ovation, he resumed his seat behind the rostrum.

Perhaps it was the climax of a lifetime for the architect who preferred landscape. But it did not seem so, to those who know him better. A few days later, he was back at the drawing board in Highgate.

This book is not a biography, although it is the story of a life devoted to design in our environment. Nor have I attempted to provide a complete documentation of his works.

What seems to me more important is to establish an accurate description of the essential achievement of this life, to record the tribulations as well as the successes. Above all, to record the background to the evolution of a new philosophy of environmental design.

This is the story of an architect who took a different path. A classicist, yet a committed modernist and idealist in the 1930s, he followed the rapids and perils of such a course, deftly steering round the rocks and currents that threatened and often sank others. Then he could be seen panning out in the calm but constraining shallows of the post-war years. A navigator, he laid out a sure course for others who favoured landscape design to follow. Four decades or more later, he might have seemed to have grounded. But spring rains came again, as they do in harsh climates, and he steered out into new and powerful currents...

With these flows, Jellicoe still runs. The maps and charts and markers he has left behind *en route* for others less skilful to follow. For now, like Mark Twain, he sets his course by intuition alone, and in that flicker of the subconscious which lies buried in each of us he finds a sure direction.

Jellicoe's path towards a design philosophy is essentially a pilgrim's progress. I have described the whole route, while the philosophy is still in the making. And increasingly I have realised that in the journey lies the secret.

It is with that objective that this book was undertaken and its conclusions reached.

Geoffrey Alan Jellicoe, c.1903, with his mother Florence Jellicoe in the garden of the Red House, Rustington, Sussex

CHAPTER 1
IN THE BEGINNING

'It is not architecture that matters. . .but rather its disposition as a part only of a landscape form'

'Landscape design is the most comprehensive of the arts. . .it is the art of the whole of man's environment'

The condition of the art of landscape, landscape design, or landscape architecture as it is known today, is commonly envisaged to be that of a transitional activity. However, as the end of the twentieth century approaches, a renaissance is underway. Landscape design, as the designing and creation of gardens in one form or another, has in various forms been pursued by man for over two and a half millennia. Wherever cities have been built, gardens of one kind or another have been established. That is this century's heritage.

Geoffrey Jellicoe, essentially a twentieth-century man, has lived throughout the century. Born in 1900, his greatest project, the Moody Historical Gardens in Galveston, is, in 1991, still under development. The primary design is completed, but he continues to work on detailed aspects, effectively finalising the numerous working drawings without which the project cannot, after his death, be realised exactly in his own terms in the twenty-first century.

Jellicoe is mindful about this consideration of time, as he has been both philosophical and phlegmatic about the vicissitudes of his art throughout his long career.

With this final project at Galveston in Texas, he has sought to express and redefine the central role that landscape as an art has always claimed in the growth of human culture and society. Although the Moody Gardens, as conceived, remain essentially a museum of landscape, the overall design incorporates Jellicoe's underlying philosophy that landscape design has to be recognised today for what it has in fact always been, the most comprehensive of the arts. In other words, contrary to general belief, it is not an art confined to private gardens and parks. It is the art of the whole of man's environment.

Jellicoe was trained as an architect, and by any standards those few projects where he has combined buildings with landcape demonstrate that, if he had concentrated on architecture rather than on landscape, he would today be equally respected for both. The restaurant at Cheddar Gorge (1934) ranks as one of the earliest essays in the international style by an English architect; light in tone and clean of line, it perfectly complements the drama of the ravine in which it sits, surely fulfilling the aspirations of his client, Lord Weymouth, himself an enlightened follower of the new style of the times. Similarly, later projects as, for example, the Grantham Crematorium and the Cheltenham Sports Centre offered articulate public buildings well related to their carefully landscaped contexts.

However, the challenge to Geoffrey Jellicoe, as the architect understood it in the 1930s, lay primarily in the clear articulation of whole environments. Those literally measured steps in Italy, as he prepared his first work, *Italian Gardens of the Renaissance,* opened new areas of perception for the architect, involving universal criteria for spatial organisation that had gradually developed in the human mind across thousands of years. Such considerations became and have remained Jellicoe's underlying preoccupations.

As a result, his career seems to defy categorising by normal criteria. He has presided as a landscape designer at the summit of his profession in the world at large, but he also helped found the formal profession of Landscape Architects in Britain (the Landscape Institute) which has become the model and basis for similar organisations in other countries. He retired officially, as he admitted in a recent interview, in 1973. At this point not only had he been President of the Institute of Landscape Architects, and Honorary President of the International Federation of Landscape Architects, but he had retired five years previously from the Royal Fine Art Commission, and 'one thought one would probably lead a quiet old age'. He was a Tate Gallery Trustee; subsequently in 1963 recognition came in the form of a CBE, and in 1979 a knighthood.

Then, at the age of eighty, 'the world, as far as I was concerned, was turned completely upside down'. To the surprise and consternation of both Geoffrey and Susan Jellicoe, two major projects arrived at his home, 19 Grove Terrace in Highgate, London. The gardens at Sutton Place, commissioned by Stanley Seeger, a Texan billionaire and enthusiast for modern art, seemed timed to throw into relief Jellicoe's whole life and work. The commission for a public park for the (communist) city authority of Modena in Italy was to prove no less challenging. In the next two years there was more to follow.

It is fortunate that Jellicoe was able to continue working through the 1980s, for it was not until then that the major transformation in contemporary thought about landscape as an art began to occur. Arguably a primary proponent of the theory that landscape design was purely transitional came from his very own profession of architects. This might seem in many respects a paradox: yet the quite revolutionary (and counter-revolutionary) developments in design philosophy concerning buildings themselves have so preoccupied the architectural world that their positioning within the environment has tended to take second place in debate. This is not to say that there have not been highly distinguished exceptions. But it was only in the late 1980s that an urgent preoccupation with environmental design in landscape began to be addressed.

Jellicoe had foreseen the need for this reappraisal many years before. However, it seems that only he has been able to set such changes clearly within a context of the arts themselves, as well as of the whole of man's culture and development.

Throughout his working life Jellicoe has continually sought out the substance of thinking about landscape (and gardens) within each historical period by reference to particular paintings of the time. Examples of the way in which he has cross-referenced one project or another with the work of different artists are numerous and will be enlarged upon throughout this study. He has repeatedly sought to resolve environmental and social conflicts, and hence to remove visual disharmony. Essentially, he designs whole environments in the way that architects design buildings. As the twenty-first century rapidly approaches, it must be said that he is closer than any other landscape designer today to establishing a working philosophy capable of resolving permanently the problems of designing man's habitat. Increasingly the solutions must relate to the environmental whole; it is not enough simply to relate buildings to the landscape. Landscape is a habitat, and architecture must be skilfully incorporated into this greater environment. The whole thrust of Jellicoe's career has been to recognise this singular truth, and to lead others to accept it.

The field was once clearly divided. In 1900, the year of Jellicoe's birth, there was garden design and there was architecture. But landscape architecture as such was not recognised to exist, any more than did the future profession of landscape architects. Garden design was essentially for gardeners. This is clear enough if we look back from 1900 to consider the prevalent ideas of the late nineteenth century. William Robinson's *The English Flower Garden*[1] virtually drove out architectural influence from the English gardener's domain: for example, both Paxton's Crystal Palace and Barry's formal designs at Shrublands were denigrated, and pergolas, palisades and topiary were likewise taboo. By 1890, formalism was distinctly out of fashion. In that year Henry Ernest Milner had published *The Art and Practice of Landcape Gardening*, introducing the role of the 'landscape architect' to England for the first time, although architectural influences were still proscribed. To architects, however, it seemed as if the disciples of Robinson, in their obsession with flowers, had joined the followers of Milner to draw a ring around those architects who dared intervene in landscape; Milner's style was gentle enough, but his message was lethal in denying architects their natural scope for layout and setting. If John Dando Sedding in *Garden Craft Old and New*[2] had been more expressive of his sympathy for a more formal approach to garden design within the Arts and Crafts movement, it would have carried an influence that was more than purely historical.

Yet the structured space maintained its hegemony in garden design. The careful precepts and guidelines laid down by the Arts and Crafts movement for garden layouts were already superbly catalogued by Thomas Mawson in *The Art and Craft of Garden Making*.[3] The garden Mawson designed in the Lake District, Graythwaite Hall, for example, bore out his remarkable skill in maintaining a degree of formalism close to the house itself, while allowing nature to approach by degrees away from the house into the middle ground.

Mawson was already laying claim not only to the master role in landscape architecture, but also to the creative leadership in planning and co-ordination of the environment. Appropriately, he was himself later to become the first president of the institution which he helped Jellicoe to found for the new profession.

Soon a further wave of energy surged through this watershed in landscape gardening in the shape of such publications as *Country Life* and *The Studio*. The

1 *The English Flower Garden*. William Robinson, first published 1883, fifteenth edition John Murray, 1933.
2 *Garden Craft Old and New*. John Dando Sedding, London, 1891.
3 *The Art and Craft of Garden Making*. Thomas H Mawson, London, 1900.

editor of *The Studio,* Charles Holme, saw himself as a mediator between the popular naturists amongst landscape gardeners and the revivalists for the structured space. In 1907 he wrote in *The Studio:*

> The landscape gardeners of today are not afflicted with the delusion that they can or should model themselves upon popular painters and plant compositions which will reproduce pictures shown at the National Gallery or the Academy. They do not merely refuse to draw inspiration from the canvases of Claude or Poussin, they seek suggestions from nature direct and try to keep in their work something of her spontaneity and charming irregularity.

The formalists received an accolade on the same page:

> The main purpose of it all is to reintroduce into modern gardens the quiet dignity and the sober richness of the seventeenth century design, without closing the way to those ingenious designers who can give new meaning and an increased significance to their combinations of the materials used by their predecessors.[4]

Holme was keeping his options open.

The division of interest led to a form of peaceful coexistence, while the Arts and Crafts movement lent credibility to numerous owner-designer produced garden plans which emerged to grace the Edwardian heyday. Nonetheless it took all the innovative skills of the architect Reginald Blomfield to convey the value of formal structured spaces, as had been common until the eighteenth century developments by Brown and Repton. To Blomfield, garden design was an essential part of 'the great art of architecture' and in 1901, in the third edition of *The Formal Garden in England,* [5] he came back at the landscape architects/gardeners on a most telling point: he claimed they had neither theory nor art. Blomfield could counter the attack on architects by practical example too: the formal yet grand design proposed at Mellerstain for Lord Binning is a characteristic masterpiece (1910). Perhaps it was Charles Voysey, however, whose architectural approach to garden design most amply vindicates the involvement of his profession in these debates and arguments — essentially a kind of Victorian demarcation dispute, or so it seems today. Voysey's remarkable eye for detail (each aspect of every fitting) was carried through into the gardens of houses like New Place, Surrey (1897) or Oakhurst, Sussex (1901), by subtly deploying the device of strong planting to make the essential link between new house and raw garden.

Most significantly, it was a chance meeting with Voysey that helped the eighteen year old Geoffrey Jellicoe to decide on entry to the Architectural Association with a view to qualifying as an architect.

The setting for Jellicoe's childhood in our story is a propitious one in which the Arts and Crafts influence is still prevalent. The twentieth century has barely run its first decade; the long Edwardian summer is still in swing.

Jellicoe's parents had a sense of fashion and style. His father was a publisher, conventional and not in the end very successful. His mother, a strong and resilient

4 'The Gardens of England', *The Studio,* Special Number, 1907.
5 *The Formal Garden in England,* Reginald Blomfield and Inigo F Thomas (illustrations), first edition London, 1892.

character, had been educated on the Continent, developed an early obsession with Wagner (she took herself to Bayreuth at the age of nineteen), and attended the Slade under Professors Tonks and Brown. She had a nomadic strain, testified to by Jellicoe, and claimed that she had moved house nineteen times in the first nineteen years of marriage.

Jellicoe had been born a Victorian, in Chelsea, but before he was two his parents had settled at the Red House in the coastal village of Rustington, near Littlehampton, behind Arundel in Sussex. Three years later, the Jellicoes built Willows (adjoining the Red House), and it was here that Jellicoe had his first experience of a landscaped garden. Designed by a respected architect in the advanced taste of the time, and under the influence of Blomfield, it nonetheless had added effects: the fore and aft conventional gardens (designed by his father) were accompanied by a narrow wilderness, designed by Mrs Jellicoe, where a grass chinoiserie path worked its way along in tightening curves.

That was his first awareness of landscape gardening: but Jellicoe's experience of landscape was all around at that age. Rustington itself lies some four miles south of the Sussex Downs. His childhood days were spent in a world bounded on one side by superb rolling hills, and on the other, five minutes walk from home, by the great expanse of shingled shore which stretched with measured perspective into the distance to Littlehampton on one side and Worthing on the other, and was punctuated by jagged lines of timber breakwaters. Against these elements, the comforting detailing of the houses in Rustington maintained a domestic scale of hearth and home. Jellicoe's sketches summarise that duality of scale. Just to the north of neighbouring Littlehampton rose the great mass of Arundel castle, the feudal core of this historic landscape habitat.

The third house inhabited by the Jellicoe family at Rustington, The Vinery, was acquired in 1913. This house faced south and was reached through a doorway in the main street of the village: but from that point on a different world existed. The house led to a veranda running along the south elevation. Significantly, the house looked on to rising ground, a gradual incline southwards, and Jellicoe claims that this situation influenced him always to prefer buildings not to be superimposed on the landscape (ie not dominant) but *of* the landscape. And The Vinery itself, as Jellicoe puts it, 'dripped with grapes'. A central path led away to the end of the garden (of which both side boundaries were hedges), across a bridge and beyond to a tennis court created from open fields. This was reached through a canopy of orchard trees after which the path suddenly emerged into the bright coastal light off the sea. Jellicoe admits that it was not until later in his professional career that he appreciated the extent to which The Vinery had influenced him subconsciously. The house lay hull-down, a secondary element within the landscape to which it belonged. Nature was paramount.

It was an extraordinary balance of the universal and the particular. Every home, however small, can be similarly protected against publicity and wind; the sun can be trapped and house and garden joined in summer flowers and scents; mystery obtained by tree and foliage planting. The Vinery showed

Willows, Rustington, c 1905, front elevation. This was the house built by Jellicoe's parents, where he had his first experience of a landscaped garden

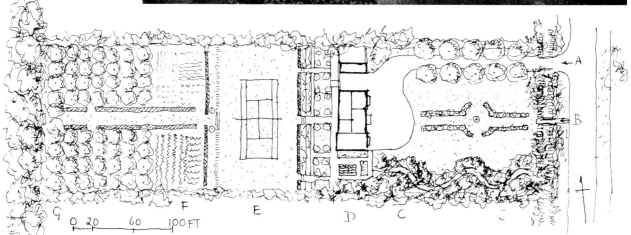

Plan of Willows, c 1905, drawn from memory by Geoffrey Jellicoe in 1988. A Drive entrance; B Garden entrance; C Wilderness; D House, fish pond and flower garden; E Tennis court; F Kitchen gardens; G Orchard

that it is not architecture that matters, for it was undistinguished, but rather its disposition as a part only of a landscape of form. Where there are eccentricities — and there usually are — enrich yourself with them as we were by the figs, the grapes, the mount, and the two staircases. . .

Revisiting The Vinery shortly before his eighty-eighth birthday was an interesting experience for Jellicoe. Both house and garden were, of course, substantially changed, yet recognisable. While the orientation to the deep garden through the south-facing veranda was much the same, the garden, although well planted up, had been truncated, to allow development at the rear. Enclosure had occurred where freedom and mystery might have stayed. Jellicoe's mind was sharp as ever to spot changes and deletions without discouraging the present occupants. The balminess of an Edwardian coastal village had been replaced by the scent of

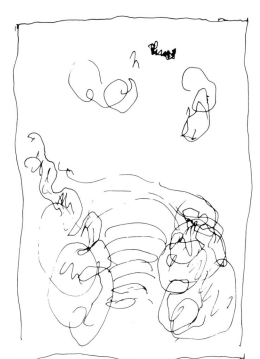

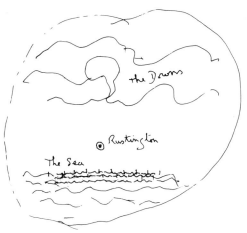

Drawing by Jellicoe of the beach and downs as a childhood habitat

Downland landscape behind Rustington drawn by Jellicoe in 1988

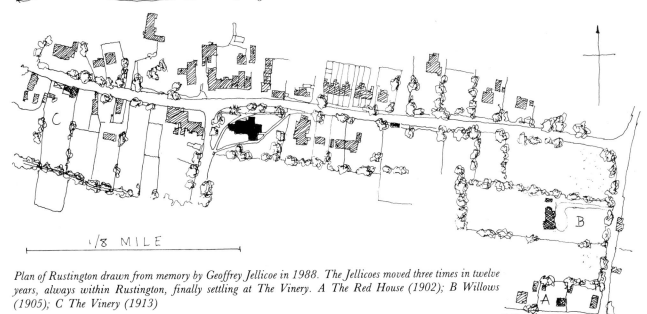

Plan of Rustington drawn from memory by Geoffrey Jellicoe in 1988. The Jellicoes moved three times in twelve years, always within Rustington, finally settling at The Vinery. A The Red House (1902); B Willows (1905); C The Vinery (1913)

overweaning prosperity. From The Vinery we walked round to the beach. There, in the late February sunlight, and only then, did Jellicoe feel recharged with enthusiasm: the solid timber breakwaters suddenly appeared as we mounted the shingle, a perspective in either direction that stretched seemingly to infinity. That singularity was unchanged.

About six months after this visit to Rustington, Jellicoe wrote:

I visited the spot outside the sitting room window of the Red House where, aged two, there began my first memory; this ordinary Edwardian house, from which, aged five, I saw being built the grand new house from the back windows [Willows]. Although surrounded by buildings, the house itself was unchanged. No emotions were aroused. I think the greatest influence must

The first landscape drawing by Sir Geoffrey Jellicoe, drawn during the summer holiday of 1908 and dedicated to his father. Note the lighthouse

The Vinery, c 1915, the third house inhabited by the Jellicoes in Rustington

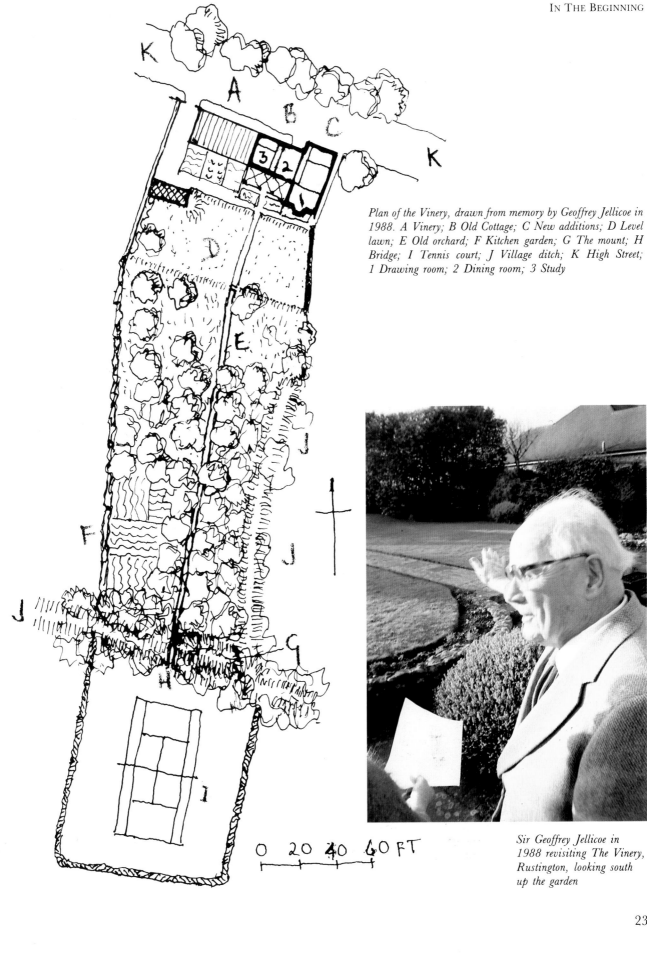

Plan of the Vinery, drawn from memory by Geoffrey Jellicoe in 1988. A Vinery; B Old Cottage; C New additions; D Level lawn; E Old orchard; F Kitchen garden; G The mount; H Bridge; I Tennis court; J Village ditch; K High Street; 1 Drawing room; 2 Dining room; 3 Study

O   20 40   60 FT

Sir Geoffrey Jellicoe in 1988 revisiting The Vinery, Rustington, looking south up the garden

The beach at Rustington, 1988

have been the sea shore, half a mile away.

Willows, a house and garden in the style of the Arts and Crafts movement, may have been my first landscape influence. The house remains, embedded in a new development that must equal Littlehampton in size. Turned into flats, its garden has totally disappeared under buildings which include the rear of shops and flats of the sumptuous new shopping centre. I felt no emotion, indeed was pleased that history had developed in such a scale and by and large in a civilised way. This I suppose is the creative instinct inside one that likes progression and takes in its stride the element of death when the life is not worth preserving.

The Vinery is very different. It lies along a short length of obviously preserved road leading west from the beautiful old church and what in my day was the post office. I found the garden, however, and its setting almost unchanged. I knocked on the door and entered in a few minutes. I found this very moving. Why? It was the only place in all her life that my mother had felt to be hers.

The garden led uphill away from the house, the eye disappearing into a rather complicated orchard. Although the site was narrow it was totally private, and everywhere gave a sense of mystery. At the far end, a view to the sea, but my mother always maintained that you should not always live with a view, but that a view should be obtainable from some part of the garden.

We loved it — the sun, the mystery of enclosure, and a short walk away the grandeur of the beaches and the marvellous rhythm of the breakwaters.

At some time when completing *Italian Gardens of the Renaissance* I went into this garden on a still summer's night. . .the sky was clear and lit up with stars. I realised that the soul within was greater than the infinity of space around one; and this moment has always been with me.

After writing these notes, and then having discarded them as too 'sloppy', I had opened my copy of Jung at random, and read the following in the Glossary:

'If the human soul is anything it must be of unimaginable complexity and diversity, so that it cannot possibly be approached through a mere psychology of instinct. I can only gaze with wonder and awe at the depths and heights of our psychic nature. Its non-spatial universe conceals an untold abundance of images which have accumulated over millions of years of living development and become fixed in the organism. My consciousness is like an eye that penetrates to the most distant spaces, yet it is the psychic non-ego that fills them with non-spatial images. And these images are not pale shadows, but tremendously powerful psychic factors... Beside this picture I would like to place the spectacle of the starry heavens at night for the only equivalent of the universe within is the universe without; and just as I reach this world through the medium of the body, so I reach that world through the medium of the psyche'.

Jellicoe would become an architect. Significantly, he had never so much as drawn a doorway despite a childhood fascination with building houses. His mathematics were sound, while direct experience of the construction of his parents' house at Rustington, The Willows, may have guided him to a more than normal insight into architecture through a sharp boyish observation of the long-suffering architect negotiating the various aspects of domestic design with his mother.

The period at Rustington was interspersed with long visits to his grandmother's house, Woodlands, Farnham Common in Buckinghamshire and close to Burnham Beeches. Here he and his elder brother John played in a charming mid-Victorian formal garden, and here, at the age of seven and as the fourth pupil there, he joined the preparatory school where, in the established English manner, he was to remain for seven years.

In 1908 the school moved location, to Beaudesert Park at Henley-in-Arden in Warwickshire, on the superb western escarpment of the Cotswolds. Four of Jellicoe's subsequent and profound landscape experiences lie close by, all of them sources of continuing influence through his career: Stratford-on-Avon; Broadway and Chipping Campden; Cheltenham College and Pittville; and Gloucester. When he retired, his own architectural practice finally left London and homed on Pershore, ten miles west of Broadway.

At school Jellicoe gained an understanding of the classical world; Latin verse particularly was to be of significant value in later life, and he evidently possessed a strong sense of rhythm and scansion. In 1913 his mother took him to Paris for an important spring fortnight:

...where breakfasts in bed, of pre-war French coffee, rolls and butter, are intermingled in memory with a glorious revelation of architecture — Notre Dame, the Louvre, Versailles, Malmaison and as much else as could be squeezed into so short a time.

Other influences, stemming from school again, were an awareness of the strength

25

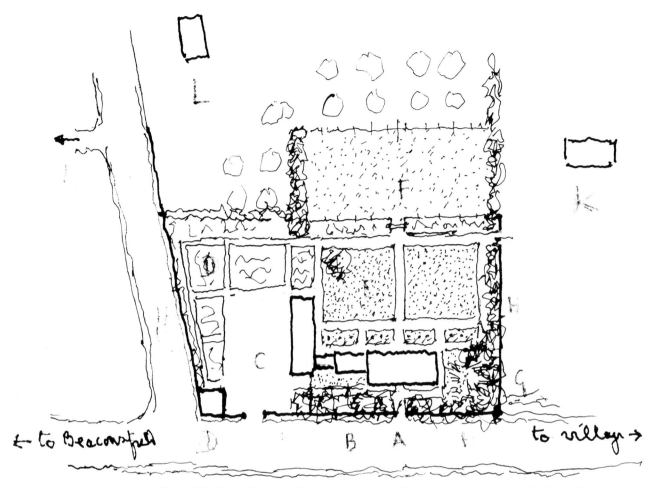

Plan of Woodlands, Farnham Common, Buckinghamshire, drawn from memory by Geoffrey Jellicoe in 1988. A House; B Studio; C Disused stable and yard/kitchen garden; D Gardener's cottage; E Lawn with mulberry tree; F Paddocks; G Romantic dell; H High brick wall

of spirituality through religion, which fused with an early feeling for 'genius loci' gained from the subtly varied essence of the South Downs. At Cheltenham College, where he gained an exhibition, however, the emphasis was on 'joining in', and Jellicoe proved himself highly adaptable, despite less than average stature: 'Quite early I found the smell of the Rugby scrum intolerable and became a wing three-quarter, so was repeatedly saved this experience by a lucky turn of speed'.

Jellicoe also remembers 'the great white circle' of the cricket field:

> I would enter this magic circle with my bat under my arm. Round the circle's edge stood or sat the whole school of some six hundred boys and masters. Playing first wicket down, I fixed my gloves and proceeded nonchalantly, to a ripple of applause, to the far off wicket, with a stomach that had almost ceased to exist.

It seems that Jellicoe had emerged very much as an all-rounder, as well as a survivor, in a school regime utterly devoid in those days of any aesthetic criteria:

> Somehow it was decided that I ought to go to the Architectural Association School, and almost immediately I was interviewed by the Secretary, F R Yerbury, who had four inches of handkerchief suspended from his breast pocket, and surprisingly treated me as an equal.

Beaudesert Park, Henley-in-Arden.

REPORT ENDING *December 21st* 190*9*

Name *Geoffrey Jellicoe* Form *III (sen. boys)*

DIVINITY - - - -	*Fair*
ENGLISH:	
Composition - - -	*Very much improved.*
History - - - - -	*Much improved.*
Geography - - - -	*Poor*
CLASSICS:	
Latin - - - - -	*Doing much better.*
Greek - - - - -	
French - - - - -	*progrès mais inattentif! Grammar*
~~German~~ - - - - -	*better*
MATHEMATICS:	
Arithmetic - - - -	*Considerably improved.*
Geometry - - - -	*} has made a good start*
Algebra - - - - -	
Extra Mathematics -	
Place in Examination	*4th*
Place for Term - - -	*5th*
Final Place for Term	*5th*
General Remarks - -	*Excellent. Has improved very much in every way*

The Term begins on Thursday Jan. 20th

Signed *A. H. Richardson*

Beaudesert Park School report, December 1909

Geoffrey Jellicoe, aged ten, at Beaudesert Park School

On the first day of term, Geoffrey Jellicoe duly entered the establishment where successively over twenty years he would be student, studio master, principal and finally member of the Council.

In the summer of 1921, Jellicoe spent part of the vacation systematically exploring London armed with sketchbook, sandwiches, and sixpence per day for the bus. The resulting drawings reflect an earlier endeavour in style and content — the task of copying out the illustrations of Banister Fletcher's *History of Architecture* from beginning to end. Although he only reached the chapter dealing with ancient Rome, the exercise had made its mark. The subsequent sketchbook pages he made of London buildings range far and wide, from church details to numerous towers, masonry details, interiors, exteriors, plans, perspectives, elevations (see pages 28 and 29). The draughtsmanship shows signs of Jellicoe's later fluidity, the sense of perspective is flawless, as is the relation of perspective to accompanying plan in the established Banister Fletcher format. To a contemporary eye, the freer renderings are the most satisfying. The only site survey (tucked away at the rear of the book) demonstrated that when Jellicoe is thinking with his pen, as opposed simply to recording what he sees, nothing has greatly changed in seventy years: and when he is thinking in plan; buildings and the space around and beyond them become one entity.

In the early 1920s the Architectural Association school was full bent on neo-classicism. The quality of technical expertise in drawing and rendering was one which aspired to Beaux-Arts standards. As Jellicoe reflects: 'I was to realise later

One of the first architectural studies, St Bartholomew's, Smithfield, drawn in 1921 in a small lined notebook

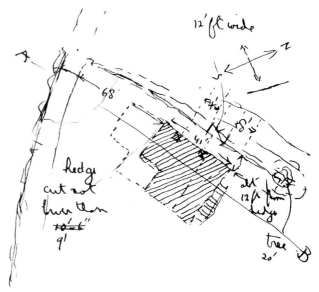

St Paul's Covent Garden, from the notebook which Jellicoe titled
Architectural Sketches & Notes

Unspecified drawing by Jellicoe; the only site survey in the notebook

that these picture-makings were the final reverberations of Claude and Poussin'. If the Architectural Association was to become in due course (and when Jellicoe was himself teaching there) a bastion of the avant-garde, the era had not yet been reached. It stood then as a repository of conservative values.

In his final year, Jellicoe competed for the Grand Prix de Rome, the renowned 'Rome prize', and was accepted for the final with three other AA students. There were six other entrants from across the country. The subject being for an heroic bridge across a ravine, Jellicoe and his successful colleagues designed in the manner of Piranesi. J C Shepherd's design, under the inspiration of the Swiss engineer Maillart, with a view to a new age, was considered to be brilliant, and when this was rejected (the winner was the Banister-Fletcher revisionist W A Cordingly, later Professor of Architecture at Manchester University) the Principal of the Architectural Association, Howard Robertson, felt obliged to challenge the result and questioned the judgement of the Royal Institute of British Architect assessors in the Association's journal. A new era in teaching had begun.

Later in 1923, Jellicoe unsuccessfully entered yet another competition, together with his fellow student J C Shepherd. Searching for a project to pursue in the year before leaving the AA, the two colleagues consulted their yearmaster, L H Bucknell, on what course of study he would advise. After delicate promptings over lunch at the Plane Tree Restaurant in Great Russell Street, he gave his considered reply: 'You should study Italian gardens, about which very little is known'.

In September 1923 the two students packed their bags, and assembled an empty portfolio, small drawing board and essential implements, and then took the boat train from Victoria, travelling light for those days of heavy baggage. In their minds, too, they abandoned the accumulated baggage of a tiresome twentieth century school curriculum, and strode easily into the world of the past.

The twelfth century castle at Carcassonne, France, which Jellicoe and Shepherd visited on their way to Italy in 1923

CHAPTER 2
THE ITALIAN
RENAISSANCE GARDENS

*'All Italian gardens are geometric and their beauty lies largely in the
reconciliation of the. . .ordered mind of man searching for
its objective with the waywardness of nature'*

Only once before had Geoffrey Jellicoe set out on an architectural tour — the
survey of London buildings which he had made in 1921. The Italian journey,
from which he returned in 1924, was on an altogether different dimension. It was
to be followed later by a second tour, in 1930, following the award of the
Architectural Association's Bernard Webb studentship. On both occasions, Italy
was to be the focus, the mainspring of his inspiration through life, up to and
including the return there in 1980 to carry out commissions for Modena and
subsequently, in 1989, for Turin.

Jellicoe and Shepherd travelled third class through France, passing through the
Loire valley and spending a night in the castle at Carcassone. But they were not
to be long diverted. They were well-briefed, having studied all available literature
and theses on Italian gardens before leaving London. As Bucknell had told them,
the study of Italian gardens had been neglected, and very little comprehensive
work had been done for many years; here, therefore, was a great and timely
opportunity to make a major contribution to knowledge.

En route, Jock Shepherd had shown Jellicoe, for the first time, how to sketch
without relying on 'bluz', identifiable as Jellicoe's own form of expressionism;
such a personal style was already identifiable in the early sketches of London
buildings but, as Shepherd rightly surmised, was not appropriate to the practical
delineation of architecture which called for exactness. Shepherd himself was a
highly skilled draughtsman who had broken away from the Beaux-Arts traditions.

A side effect of Shepherd's proficiency seems to have been Jellicoe's further
conviction, highly mistaken as it turns out, that he himself could not draw
effectively. This was to be dramatically disproved in later years. In any event,
Jellicoe carried out the surveys from now on, and Shepherd executed the superb
plans, elevations and sections of Italian villas and gardens which were soon to be
published in all their glory.

> After skirmishing with the Palladian villas in the Veneto and following in the
> pacings of diarist John Evelyn at the Villa Valmarana, Vicenza, we made our
> leisurely way to the Mecca of Italian Gardens — Florence.[1]

There, through a contact of Jellicoe's mother, and a close friend of Bernard
Berenson, the two students were introduced to a network of garden enthusiasts.
They met the English architect Cecil Pinsent (whose baroque decoration at Villa

1 Jellicoe Papers, Casebook,
unpublished.

J C Shepherd, left. Fellow student, and co-author with Jellicoe of Italian Gardens of the Renaissance, *Shepherd had been badly wounded during the First World War and subsequently received an MC*

Villa Corsi-Salviati, Sesto (1637-60). 'The long narrow garden lies sparkling with its rich variety: brilliant green parterre dotted with statues, fountains, flowing walls and imposing gateways, and more statues. Nowhere can the eye rest without wanting to dash off to something new . . . Even the house, forgetting its own medley of buildings, throws a genial front on the riot and exuberantly joins the fun. Everywhere flows the spirit of life and gaiety. The wonder is that although the garden suggests unlimited length, its infinite number of features are crowded into quite a small space'

I Tatti had not pleased Kenneth Clark), designer of some skilfully integrated new housing on the highly sensitive slopes below Fiesole, and it was Pinsent who gave Jellicoe his first lesson in distant landscape.

> One of our earliest targets was the Villa Medici at Fiesole...Despite the persistently noisy separation of the sole from my right shoe as we entered the great salon to be received, we were given permission to measure the gardens provided we were out by 8 a.m.[2]

The owners here were English: Lady Sybil Scott[3] and her husband Geoffrey Scott, author of an outstanding work, *The Architecture of Humanism*.[4]

Jellicoe found the English deeply entrenched around Florence, and had been for decades:

> We must for instance have been the first visitors actually ever to have walked up the avenue of La Pietra, the home of Arthur Acton, for I recall seeing two small white statues facing each other on either side of the distant entrance, and only by slow degrees realising that they were huge aproned footmen waiting our arrival.[5]

The Florentine owners, however, responded with even greater hospitality to the oddly persistent English pair. The aristocratic proprietor of the Villa Corsi-Salviati insisted on being given a copy of the drawings, but in exchange made available a large network of his extended family and its various connections.

> A cousin...took us by public tram to his villa, Poggio Torselli, where we walked uninhibited up the avenue together to an al fresco lunch.[6]

The al fresco lunch subsequently became an essential formula in Geoffrey Jellicoe's own hospitality, as many friends and acquaintances can acknowledge.

As the surveys of the gardens contained within the fertile triangle of Florence-Lucca-Sienna proceeded apace, Jellicoe became increasingly fascinated (literally with every step) by the clearly sequential nature of the spaces, and so by the realisation on the drawing-board of 'proportioned shapes and then in the meaning of those shapes'. Early in his schooldays he had learnt the potential of geometry, of the triangle, by thinking not of the lines, but of the space within: now this childhood awareness of the 'absolute, finite and infallible nature of Euclid' came back to him in full flood.

> All Italian gardens [of the Renaissance] are therefore geometric and their beauty lies largely in the reconciliation of the up-surging, logical, scientific, and ordered mind of man searching for its objective, with the waywardness of nature. The basic materials are grey stone, gravel walks, clipped evergreens, and water: materials which are soft and cool to the senses, but like those of architecture, unchanging with the seasons. There was no accepted place for flowers, not so much because the climate was unsuitable, as that they formed no part in the scheme of things. In ideas there were only two parties concerned in gardens: man and the universe; and nature in any other form except as a kindly provider of materials would have been an intrusion.[7]

2 Ibid.
3 See *Tuscan Villas*, Harold Acton, Thames & Hudson, 1973. 'Lady Sybil was eccentric by modern standards...something of the Platonic Academy still lingered in her day at the Villa Medici'.
4 *The Architecture of Humanism*, Geoffrey Scott, second edition, London, 1924.
5 Jellicoe Papers, Casebook, unpublished.
6 Ibid.
7 Jellicoe Papers, unpublished notes.

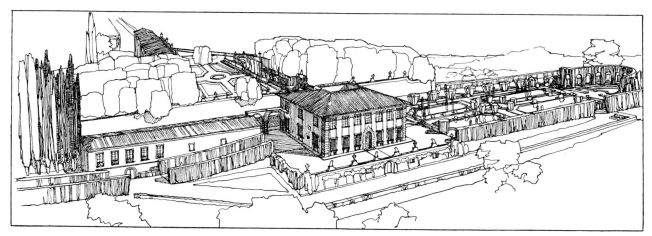

Villa Gamberaia, Settignano (c 1610). 'Probably still the most interesting garden existing where all the various aspects of the individual mind find their counterpart in the physical environment... The house of the Villa Gamberaia, now mellowed to a soft ivory colour and perfectly embodying the Tuscan ideal of restraint and proportion, is the centre of a garden that varies with every aspect...there is a place for every mood'

If Tuscany could offer such a wide range of versatility in garden design encompassing differing solutions for each individual garden and so reflecting the aspiration of each proprietor (a perfect example being Gamberaia), it was Rome that remained the principal and ultimate inheritor of the classical tradition, and most especially its characteristic scale. To Jellicoe, the journey from Florence to Rome was a journey of escalating grandeur. It was only long after that he realised it was also a voyage backwards in time, from the modern to the ancient world:

> The one was an awakening of the spirit of individuality in landscape and was to have a profound effect on my distant future: the other was a rebirth of antique Rome, practised almost entirely by the Church, and its influence was to be equally profound, but indirect and abstract. Subconsciously I...shied away from the greater Roman gardens.[8]

Jellicoe found that in Florence humanism had been a form of intellectual awakening that sought confirmation from Greece and ancient Rome direct, and not from the authority of the Church. In Florence the Medici circle saw itself inheriting the role of the Platonic Academy, a model for the rebirth of the way of life the Florentines knew only from Pliny and Horace. Jellicoe saw this Roman/Florentine dichotomy as marked typically by the work of Michelozzo Michelozzi at Cafaggiolo (1451),[9] still essentially a medieval fortress with a formal and compartmented garden (see page 38). Yet Michelozzi's design for the Villa Medici so soon afterwards (1458-61) had, he saw, provided the first truly Renaissance villa. The house runs along the hillside, offering open perspectives through which the still formal gardens embrace the surroundings. Jellicoe was to return frequently in later projects to the idea of the embodiment of philosophy into a garden's role and function.

In and around Rome, Jellicoe and Shepherd persevered with their task:

> The villas of Frascati appealed to us at the time more than Este, for we

8 Jellicoe Papers, Casebook, unpublished.
9 Commissioned by Cosimo de Medici to remind the family of their earlier medieval descent.

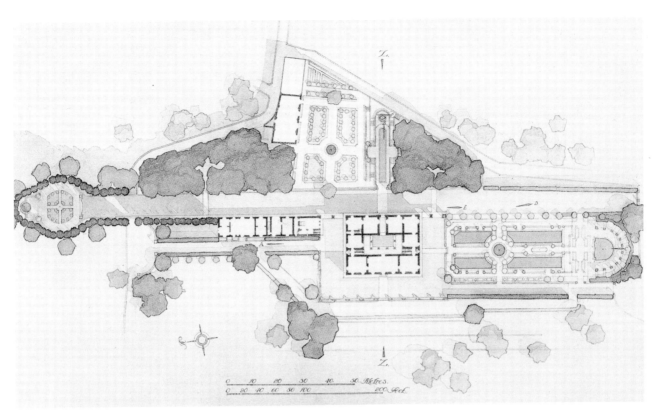

Villa Gamberaia, plan

Villa Gamberaia, section and elevation

*Villa Medici, Fiesole (1458-61, Michelozzo Michelozzi). 'One of the many country residences of the great
Lorenzo [it] brings home very forcibly the life of entertaining associated with that Florentine school of thought,
the Platonic Academy... There is probably as much dignity of learning expressed in the long simple lines of
the terraces cut out of the hills below Fiesole, as there ever was in all the cultivated arguments promoted within
its precincts. As one of the buildings, therefore, which mark the dawn of the Renaissance, and in which the
newly born love of art and freedom were fostered and spread abroad, the Villa has a special interest'*

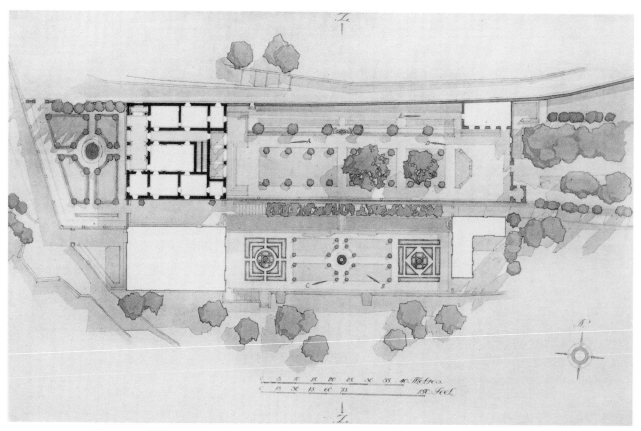

Villa Medici, Fiesole, plan

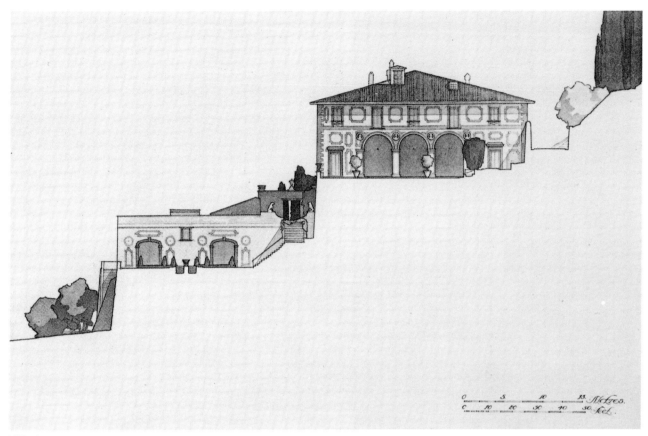

Villa Medici, Fiesole, section

appreciated that here was a complex of grand landscapes that made a curiously homogeneous whole. It was here that we had our only conflict with authority, for except for an alarming attack by guard dogs near Lucca, who had shot us out of the garden with our teeth chattering, we had never actually been refused entrance. We had seen and admired two Alinari views of the Villa Piccolomini, but had heard of the owner's absolute refusal of entry. We called, were taken to the family in the garden, and were refused permission. Since the basic shape is no more than a rectangle, I believed that if I could take only a few dimensions, the plan could be reconstructed from the photographs. While Jock argued in broken Italian, I paced; and since this lovely villa was destroyed in the war, it may be that our Machiavellian approach was justified and helped in its reconstruction.[10]

So accurate had been Jellicoe's pacing, that little adjustment was needed when the superb plan and elevation were included in the study:

The long walls of clipped ilex, the burst of view either side of the house, and the rich carpet of parterre, all give to the garden the effect of being the stately salon of a great family.[11]

10 Jellicoe Papers, Casebook, unpublished.
11 Jellicoe Papers, unpublished notes.

Seventeenth century hunting scene. The Medici castle at Cafaggiolo, north of Florence, by Michelozzo Michelozzi (1451), with its medieval fortress and compartmented garden, characterised for Jellicoe the difference between Roman and Florentine Renaissance villas

Villa Piccolomini, Frascati (c 1560). 'The blending of house and garden so completely has produced a peaceful harmony of thought'

Jellicoe was struck by the idea of the outdoor room, and would return in later projects to this idea, not least at Sutton Place and in the final project for the Moody Historical Gardens.

In fact, some fourteen schemes were surveyed by Shepherd and Jellicoe around Rome itself, and a further five at Frascati; and, of course, they excluded as yet the Villa d'Este at Tivoli. The latter they had indeed visited, but with the self-justification of true students, declared it 'truly decadent'. (Subsequently this garden was included in the book at second hand, with the central axis shown (wrongly) at right angles to the terraces, instead of in the correct 'askew' alignment.)

It is hard to understand the significant reasons for this initial rejection: what d'Este lacks in humanism through its excessively formal garden arrangement (notwithstanding the skew), it compensates for in the sophisticated manner by which the element of water, a favourite device of Jellicoe's, is articulated playfully throughout the scheme.

Possibly Geoffrey Jellicoe's own awareness of the importance of water in landscape only really developed later. But (like Cecil Pinsent's adaptation of the Villa Papiniano at Fiesole and its superb garden (1925) — a 'Roman' Villa in Florence[12]) at Villa d'Este it was the combination of gradient and water that had so delighted the English in Florence which was in turn communicated to Jellicoe.

By contrast, it is precisely Vignola's ennoblement of the Villa Lante's exotic but hedonistic spread of formalised terraces at Bagnaia that earns the highest praise in

12 The Villa Papiniano gardens had been restored and redesigned for Hugh S Whitaker by Cecil Pinsent and were completed in 1925. Previously Pinsent rebuilt I Tatti and redesigned the garden for Bernard Berenson, 1908-15.

Villa Papiniano, Florence. The architect Cecil Pinsent exploited the combination of gradient and water which so delighted the English in Florence and later Jellicoe

Villa d'Este, Tivoli (1550, Pirro Ligorio). 'The river was spread through the gardens, split into varying notes, and the whole place throbs to the sound, here rising to a thunder, there sinking to a drone. The architecture echoes the music in the variety of its tones. There is the grandeur of the water organ stretching its white tongue down to the pools and the staccato notes of countless fountains scattered abroad'

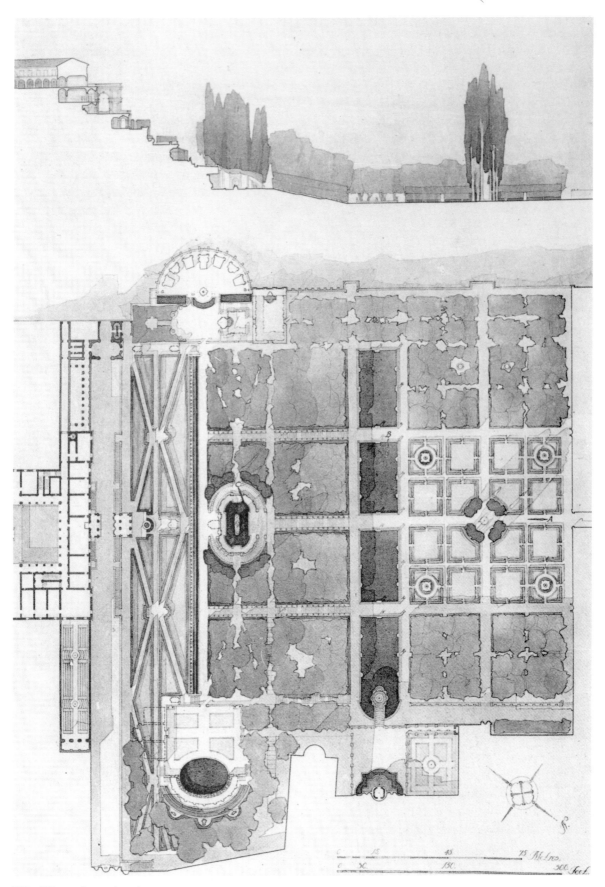

Villa d'Este, plan and section

Villa d'Este, the north elevation from a photograph by Alinari

Jellicoe's *Studies in Landscape Design* (1960). Here, latterly, Geoffrey Jellicoe redeems the Villa d'Este as the most important Roman Renaissance garden:

> It is overwhelmingly impressive not only for its architecture, its disposition and even its somewhat robust and crude detail, but also for the sound of its waters which, to the visitor walking around it, varies like the tone of a gigantic organ.[13]

13 *Studies in Landscape Design,* vol 1, OUP, 1960, p6.

Villa Lante, Bagnaia (begun 1564, Vignola). 'Finality and perfection in pure classical garden planning were reached in the curious and original Villa Lante at Bagnaia . . . It contains the elements of the Perugino picture ['Christ Giving the Keys to St Peter', see page 44], the place of the domed building being taken by the parterre and Giovanni da Bologna's fountain, and that of the classical arches by square twin houses'

It is evident that the garden of the Villa Lante is an indirect translation of Perugino's 'Christ Giving the Keys to St Peter' (Sistine Chapel, 1503). It is clear, too, that the presence of elements of Perugino's work in the Villa Lante was a significant factor for Jellicoe when he bestowed the accolade of perfection in pure classical garden planning upon the Villa Lante, this 'most contemplative of all gardens'.

For Jellicoe, *Italian Gardens of the Renaissance* was a student project first and foremost. But the lessons acquired on that painstaking and methodical research (upon which Jellicoe later admitted to doing all the ground work) took him many years longer to assimilate. And while the prompt and successful publication of the book by Sir Ernest Benn in 1925 gave an immediate boost to his professional career, there is little in the text that fully reveals the extent of·those assimilated ideas and measures. The true rewards of that venture appeared, stage by stage, very much later. In due course, later publications by Jellicoe, such as the three volumes of *Studies in Landscape Design* [14] and *Water: The Use of Water in Landscape Architecture*, [15] as well as the major work *The Landscape of Man* [16] (both the last with

14 Ibid, vol 1 1960, vol 2 1966, vol 3 1970.
15 *Water: The Use of Water in Landscape Architecture,* Geoffrey and Susan Jellicoe, London, 1971.
16 *The Landscape of Man,* Geoffrey and Susan Jellicoe, London and New York, 1975.

Perugino's painting of 'Christ Giving the Keys to St Peter'

Villa Lante, section of the main pool photographed by Moscioni

Susan Jellicoe), indicate clearly the nature and extent of that learning experience; and finally, in several of his later landscape projects, it becomes especially clear. The truth is that Jellicoe, in his research on the Italian landscape gardens of the Renaissance, began to realise his bent, still latent, for the articulation of open space landscape, water and garden. In the process, he became a designer of landscapes, as distinct from pure architecture. It was a subconscious transition.

Villa Lante, Bagnaia. The rill. 'A perfect thing of the imagination'

Villa Lante, Bagnaia. The parterre

46

Steps in Gordon Russell's garden at Chipping Campden, Gloucestershire, 1929. The project to accommodate changes of level proved extremely successful

CHAPTER 3
EARLY PROJECTS

'Conceiver, author and stage designer of a social mise-en-scène, *so placed in the landscape to please that the world remembered'*

Following their return to England, Jellicoe and Shepherd were in partnership for some eight years. Jock Shepherd, whose career at the Architectural Association school had been one of uninterrupted distinction, returned there to teach part time. In 1926 the partners designed a garden for Sir Ernest Benn, and in 1927 Jellicoe was selected by Avray Tipping, then architectural editor of *Country Life,* to be introduced to a prospective client wishing to improve and restore Claremont in Surrey, formerly the home of Clive of India. Although the Claremont project never materialised, it was there that Tipping one day introduced Jellicoe to Christopher Hussey, later Tipping's successor at *Country Life.* Jellicoe was getting better known. Soon after, as Jellicoe recalls:

> I opened the office door at 60 York Terrace to a tall, youngish visitor, wearing a new Homburg hat. He introduced himself as Gordon Russell, declared that *Gardens and Design* [Jellicoe's second publication for Benn] was the best garden book he had read, and invited me to come to his home near Chipping Campden for the day. We agreed a date. On a perfect summer's day I sat in a recently made terraced garden overlooking one of the most beautiful views I had known, Italy not excepted. With the Russells I cogitated on things in general, then I caught the evening train home. It seemed at the time, no more than an enjoyable excursion, yet Gordon Russell, as Christopher Hussey, was to influence me profoundly in the beginnings of my own later practice.

In 1929 Jellicoe took over from Jock Shepherd as a master at the Architectural Association school. Concurrently came the first moves towards the establishment of the Institute of Landscape Architects. Jellicoe played an important part in this process which led to the formal constitution of the Institute as a body in 1929. Thomas Mawson was the first president, and Jellicoe, without opposition (there were just enough members to form a quorum) appointed himself editor of the quarterly *Notes.*

The Architectural Association played a central role for Jellicoe for some years from 1929 onwards. With three masters to sixty students, it was a demanding enough task which he entered into with relish, primarily because it involved teaching over the drawing board. The period up to 1939 was a critical one in the development of modern British architecture, for it was a time when new developments on the Continent began somewhat erratically to take root in the

British Isles, and in circumstances that were quite incidental to national life and culture. Numerous of Jellicoe's students of the decade subsequently rose to fame. Living now in Highpoint I, Lubetkin's masterpiece of the period, Jellicoe enjoys pulling the leg of those former students, early modernists and now retired themselves, who live in Georgian houses today. Jellicoe himself, at least, while both traditionalist and classicist has remained a distinctive figure in the modern movement, with an unshakeable commitment to its initial ethos.

In 1930, Jellicoe was fortunate to be back in Italy, as winner of the Architectural Association's Bernard Webb studentship which covered six months travel abroad. Productive weeks were passed, first with the British School at Athens, and then the British School at Rome. As the weather warmed, Jellicoe moved northwards to begin the serious study of Austrian gardens. This resulted in *Baroque Gardens of Austria* for Victor Gollancz (at the time a director at Ernest Benn), published in 1932. Later, with the Neale Bursary of the RIBA, Jellicoe was to study the historic gardens of Germany, and this material in due course emerged many years later, in 1975, as part of *The Landscape of Man*.

At the end of September 1931, Geoffrey Jellicoe took the plunge, rented a top corner room in Bloomsbury Square at £1 a week, installed some items of family furniture, a typewriter and a telephone extension, put up his plate, and began on his own at last.

As the 1930s advanced his earlier enterprise and contacts began to convert into firmer prospects the promise that was now clearly recognised.

Gordon Russell had already discussed with Jellicoe some additions to his house and gardens at Chipping Campden, and the flight of steps Jellicoe proposed to accommodate changes of level in the garden had been singularly successful. He then proceeded to undertake, at Russell's instigation and introduction, an environmental plan for the nearby village of Broadway, Worcestershire. If Cheddar Gorge was to stand as Jellicoe's testament to the new spirit of modernism, his remarkable project at Broadway offered an equally radical, if less emblematic statement about the future of the countryside and its buildings.

If anything, it is strongly arguable that Geoffrey Jellicoe saved the village of Broadway for posterity. His *Advisory Plan and Report for the Parish of Broadway in Worcestershire* (1933) is a model of simplicity. A fifteen page document, it contained a survey and plan of enviable clarity. In fact, it was to be the first document of its kind under the new Town and Country Planning Act (1932), and came to be considered a model for the future. That future, of course, was hard to be accurate about in 1933.

One statement stands out in italics in Jellicoe's introduction: 'The beauty of Broadway lies in its submission to the landscape; it is a stone village, and belongs to the enfolding hills'.

Broadway has for two centuries been considered to be one of the most beautiful villages in England. Symbolically, it was from Broadway Tower that William Morris addressed the letter that led to the formation of the Society for the Protection of Ancient Buildings. By the 1930s the village was coming under threat with the advent of tourism. That early twentieth century precursor of the wide-

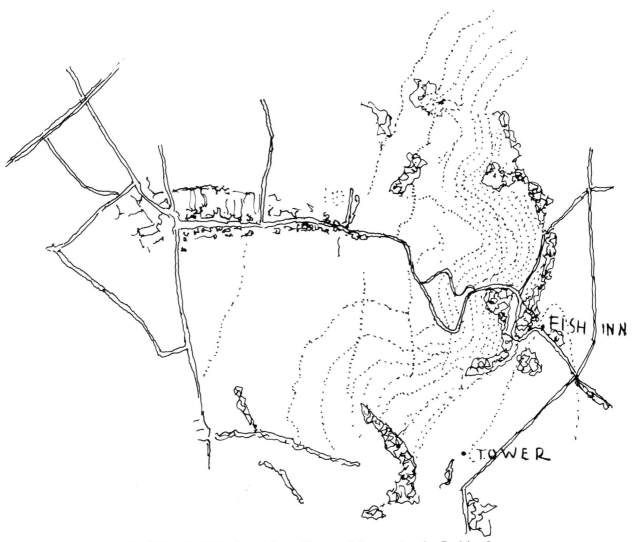

Plan of Broadway drawn by Jellicoe in 1988. In Advisory Plan and Report for the Parish of Broadway, Worcestershire *(1933), he wrote 'The beauty of Broadway lies in its submission to landscape; it is a stone village, and belongs to the enfolding hills'. Broadway village (top) is readily visible from hills to the east and Broadway Tower (bottom right)*

bodied jet, the charabanc, was becoming a problem, fair weather or foul.

Confronted with such problems, and in a community with which, through Gordon Russell (whose family firm owned the Lygon Arms hotel as well as the shop and works in Broadway), he had close ties in mind and spirit, Jellicoe's recommendations were extremely practical. Following a full survey of historical, geological and topographical factors, he proposed a plan covering zoning, planting, and special items. Within the village itself he made special recommendations covering traffic, parking, sports facilities, natural planting, and the control of building elevations and all signposting. A very useful proposal related to setting up a special trust, with a professional advisory panel, for the conservation of buildings.

The German architect Erich Mendelsohn's design for the Mosse Pavilion, Cologne (1928, top), indicates a tendency culminating, on settling in England, in the De la Warr Pavilion, Bexhill-on-Sea (1933-34, above)

Subsequently, and following collaboration in the formation of the Institute of Landscape Architects (together with Stanley Hart, Richard Sudell, Oliver Hill, Russell Page and Brenda Colvin), Sudell and Page, invited Jellicoe to undertake a joint commission for Viscount Weymouth in Somerset — the restaurant building at Cheddar Gorge.

It was this project which now placed Geoffrey Jellicoe unwittingly in the foreground of modern architecture in England at the time. His standpoint at the Architectural Association had been modernist without reservations, and Cheddar Gorge made its mark. A two-stage building project was proposed (whose progress had enabled Jellicoe to engage his own students in a parallel studio programme named Feddup Falls), and the completed scheme was well reviewed in the architectural press.

Cheddar Gorge (1934) was an inspired scheme for an intelligent and ambitious client. Lord Weymouth (now the Marquis of Bath) had a sense of style and was

A rare perspective drawing by Geoffrey Jellicoe of the landscape context of Cheddar Gorge

aware of the remarkable topography of the site. The restaurant made full use of reinforced concrete techniques little known in Britain at the time, and brought a contemporary and international flavour to bear upon a dramatic location. In this Jellicoe developed a building which, while drawing upon expressionist architecture of the period, such as that of Erich Mendelsohn in Germany, nonetheless betrayed the play of elements acquired from his classical education. Here he skilfully manipulated concrete and glass, introducing a glass-bottomed pool with fountains above and a restaurant below in a direct manner and with memorable results. Yet this modern building, unlike those of his seniors and contemporaries, nestled w[...] into the geologically challenging location. Jellicoe responded to the great vertic[...]

Cheddar Gorge, the realised project, 1934. The pool and related steps are typical Jellicoe devices

of the site with an articulate and modulated horizontality. Cheddar Gorge was a small masterpiece of its day.

Russell Page supervised the interior decoration, Jellicoe provided the architectural setting, while Gordon Russell, appropriately enough, supplied the furniture. As a multi-disciplinary team, Page, Russell and Jellicoe had achieved a remarkable success.

Undoubtedly the windfall of 1935 for Geoffrey Jellicoe was the commission for the Italian garden at Ditchley Park. It was also a milestone in his progress as a landscape architect, for it was the first in a series of important historical gardens which drew upon his unique expertise acquired through his Italian researches.

Some time following the completion of Cheddar Gorge, Ronald Tree received a recommendation from *Country Life* that Geoffrey Jellicoe was a suitable designer for a new garden for his new acquisition at Ditchley, Oxfordshire. On meeting Ronald and Nancy Tree in their London home, close to the Architectural Press at Queen Annes Gate, Jellicoe learned that the Trees each possessed their own copy of *Italian Gardens of the Renaissance,* and immediately felt more relaxed.

Ditchley Park was built between 1720 and 1724 by James Gibbs and is considered to be his domestic masterpiece. Gibbs is also universally known as the architect of the Senate House in Cambridge, and St Martin-in-the-Fields, Trafalgar Square.

Cheddar Gorge, a view to the north side of the gorge across the glass-bottomed pool, 1934

The restaurant building in Cheddar Gorge, seen from the road, 1934

Although the house was a grand exposition of architecture in the Palladian manner as developed in England in the eighteenth century, Jellicoe comments:

> Even if I had studied the Italian Renaissance Garden in considerable detail, my actual experience in classical design was non-existent. In fact I leant, in my own design and aesthetic preference, totally towards the modern movement — that was my position at the AA school where I was teaching. Putting aside my contemporary ideas of modernism, of Le Corbusier, Frank Lloyd Wright, I nonetheless entered into this historical project, history made real.

In the nineteenth century, J C Loudon had published early designs for the garden at Ditchley, deploying some of the tricks of the 'Irregular' style with its introduction of his version of the picturesque. But little stood in Jellicoe's way when he went down to survey Ditchley: 'Nothing of a garden remained. . .a path, but no gardens around'. This was a gift of providence.

Jellicoe knew that Gibbs had worked in Rome for two years in the office of the baroque architect Carlo Fontana, where he had found the influence of Bernini paramount. And, through his own experience of Roman gardens, he sympathised with Bernini's focus on space around and between objects, thus discarding the classical doctrine. Yet Jellicoe also realised that the encroachment of the ideas of the picturesque coincided with Gibbs' intentions (as indicated in the long terrace and enclosed garden shown in the 1727 plan (see page 65), but never executed).

In his plan of 1936 Jellicoe could take advantage of those never-fulfilled intentions as well as of the terms of reference in his own commission (while noting Gibbs' plan) that Ditchley should not be reconstructed simply as a historical exercise. All Jellicoe's accumulated Italian experience was brought to bear on the 1938 enclosed garden and its formal layout. The classical spirit was preserved and amplified by the creation of a landscaped terrace that served as an introduction to viewable terrain over which a classical temple stands out distantly from the surrounding woods. A previous exercise in the picturesque, carried out about fifty years after Gibbs, had ignored the concave nature of the contour to the valley and, somewhat impractically, installed a lake that would not hold water in an effort to simulate a gentle river: Jellicoe subtly lifts the eye over this disappointment to the temple beyond where the imagination can rise.

There are superficial similarities between the enclosed garden layout and its termination at Ditchley and the south garden at the Villa Gamberaia, especially as completed by the semi-circular pool. Here Jellicoe installed an ingenious water-curtain, and here, too, unobserved from the house, one could swim in shade in the cool of the evening, or wallow in the morning sun. In the formal layout, elements of the earlier Villa Piccolomini at Frascati were recalled.[1] Jellicoe had remembered Gibbs' connection with the Rome office of Carlo Fontana, but wisely foreswore the intrusion of such baroque fantasies as the Villa Cetinale of that architect (page 60): his brief was for Palladian man no less. This principle more than anything else was to be universally applied here. As Jellicoe says: 'Tree was a true Palladian with a purist instinct for the grandeur of geometric proportion'. As Tree

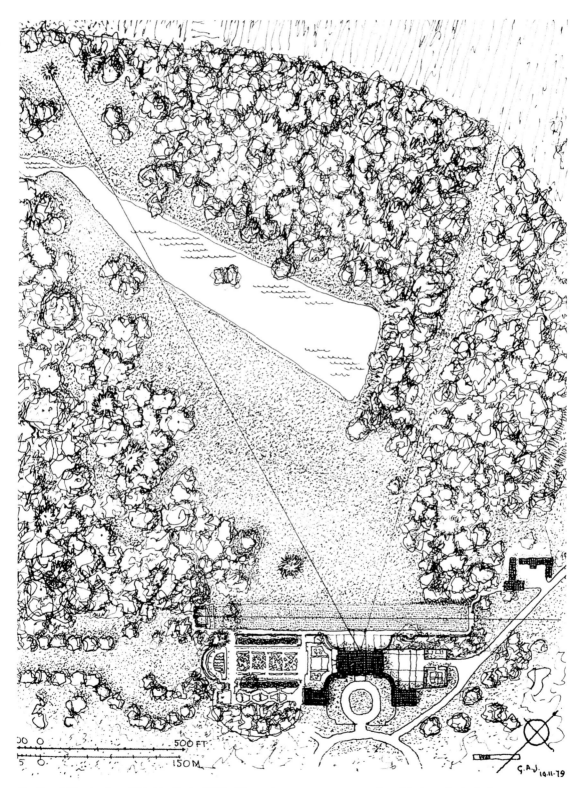

Geoffrey Jellicoe's plan of Ditchley Park, 1936. The gardens are seen as an extension of the house in the Italian manner

The South Garden of the Villa Gamberaia which influenced Jellicoe's proposals for an enclosed garden at Ditchley Park

Fountains at Ditchley Park around the semi-circular pool, both designed by Geoffrey Jellicoe

The water-curtain of secret fountains at Ditchley Park, designed by Geoffrey Jellicoe in 1936. This was an ingenious device whereby bathers could use the pool unobserved from the house

said: 'The great terrace was Jellicoe's great achievement, three hundred yards in length, it ran north and south on the west side of the house overlooking the lake'.[2]

Ditchley became alive again in the years before the Second World War, and Jellicoe found, like the very Renaissance architects he had sought to record for posterity, that he had been conceiver, author and stage designer of a social *mise-en-scène* so placed in the landscape to please that the world remembered. He became identified with the setting, above all with its successful blending of English landscape with Palladian ideals.

2 cf *When the Moon Was High: Memoirs of Peace and War 1897-1942*, Ronald Tree, 1975.

Villa Piccolomini, Frascati, a view south-east to the semi-circular pool, a further Italian influence on Geoffrey Jellicoe at Ditchley Park

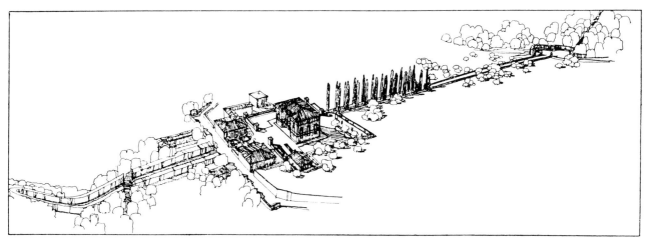

The Villa Cetinale, Sienna, designed by Carlo Fontana, 1680. Gibbs had worked in Fontana's office in Rome for two years, but if such baroque fantasies as the Villa Cetinale, with its immensely long vista, interested him on his return to England, he eschewed them at Ditchley, producing a house that was essentially High Renaissance

Jellicoe enjoyed the contrast of these two worlds. He would close the door on his small office in Bloomsbury Square and travel down from London, where he had been teaching the new spirit in architecture as demanded by the aspiring modernist students of the time (who respected him for his triumph at Cheddar Gorge), and would seem like Proust to travel back in time. Later, as if to retain a sense of proportion, and to re-emphasise the change of scale, he drew to scale on the plan of Ditchley the plan of his own modest house and garden in Grove Terrace, Highgate.

1935 was a momentous year for Jellicoe in other ways too, for that year he met Susan Pares.[3] There had been a time, in Bloomsbury Square, when with one telephone, one extension, and no secretary, Jellicoe would answer a call, as he puts it: ' "Oh yes, I'll see if Mr. Jellicoe is in" and walk across the room to the other phone and pick it up and say "Yes, Yes" '.

Practice had been a knife-edge process. But as 1935 wore on, and thanks to the Trees' commission, and others such as that at Royal Lodge, Jellicoe at last decided to advertise for a secretary. Susan walked through the door in reply, they fell in love, and were married in July 1936.

This was a time of beneficial private commissions. Following Ditchley, Jellicoe was asked by the Duke and Duchess of York (later George VI and Queen Elizabeth, now the Queen Mother) to create new gardens adjoining Royal Lodge, Windsor, Wyattville's romantic pseudo-castle to 'outcastle all others'. He addressed himself to solving the transitional zone between house ('all pink and white like an iced cake') and garden-park. A cake has to have a stand, so to speak, and Jellicoe's rapid analysis provided precisely that. A viewing 'bastion' was added, incorporating, to a playful degree, the ethos of history. Superlative trellis work was surmounted by two carved timber lions, based on the heraldry at Hampton Court. More important, a spirit of youthful celebration of the place caught the mood of the Yorks and their young daughters (the future Queen Elizabeth II and Princess Margaret). It was a successful and very private commission, but one that was to establish a long-lasting and mutual respect.

The garden at St Paul's Walden Bury has developed, as gardens should, over a protracted time scale. Set deep in the Hertfordshire countryside lies the best

3 Susan Pares was the daughter of the great Russian historian, Sir Bernard Pares. The Pares family introduced Jellicoe to an entirely scholarly world. Susan's brother Richard was a Fellow of All Souls and stayed with the Jellicoes throughout the war, influencing reading lists considerably (an essential aspect of an air raid warden's life).

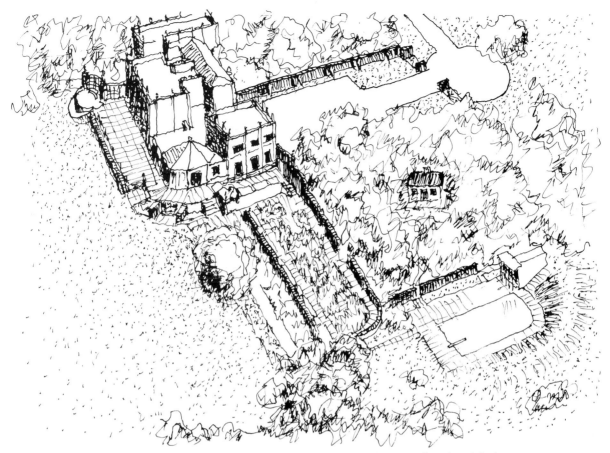

Royal Lodge, Windsor, illustrating the terraces and trellis work on a 'plinth' surrounding the original building, as designed by Jellicoe in 1936

Royal Lodge, Windsor, with Jellicoe additions, seen from Windsor Great Park

Detail of the trellis work with heraldic beasts, Royal Lodge, Windsor

remaining English garden layout in the manner of Le Nôtre. Echoing the message of Vaux-le-Vicomte, Courance, Chantilly and Versailles, it proclaims that the ultimate achievement in garden design is so to organise the surrounding lands to a house that these *predominate;* yet a web had been broken, and it had to be mended so skilfully that, with natural progress and time, the whole would be sustained. With this commission Jellicoe found himself an appointed curator of this secret landscape world, and without reservation. The process at St Paul's Walden Bury has been gradual and in humanising the park's essential geometry, temples, sculpture and a pavilion have subsequently been added. (This garden is discussed in greater detail in Chapter 10: The Contribution to Theory, pages 178-180).

At Mottisfont Abbey in Hampshire (now a National Trust property) the owners came to Jellicoe with a brief that he simplify the picturesque setting around the thirteenth century house, restore a degree of order and include a flower garden close to the main rooms and outlook. Jellicoe restored the sense of open and closed, the reconciliation of opposites that he recalled so well from visits a decade earlier to Bingham's Melcombe in Dorset. The plan as finally executed included a paved walk, leading on to a path surrounding and defining the much altered building line, which then enters a terrace of pleached limes. At the request of the owners, colour was introduced by means of ample and well-shaded herbaceous planting. Here Jellicoe strove to return the ethos of the place, and to provide a view outwards through the sixteenth century *piano nobile* which restored simplicity and breadth as well as depth of perspective.

St Paul's Walden Bury, Hertfordshire, seen from the grounds which Jellicoe was commissioned to recreate in 1936

Bingham's Melcombe, Dorset, drawn by Jock Shepherd, 1926, the inspiration for the open and closed effect which Jellicoe achieved at Mottisfont Abbey

Mottisfont Abbey, the pleached lime terrace and north facade. Jellicoe restored a sense of open and closed here, the conciliation of opposites which had influenced him a decade earlier

Plan of Mottisfont Abbey, Hampshire, 1937, redrawn by Jellicoe in 1982

James Gibbs' plan of 1727 of Ditchley Park. The house and approach areas are clearly visible, as is the proposed long terrace which would fix the building against the falling contours that skew the site

Seat and surrounds at Ditchley, designed by Jellicoe in 1936 to accommodate sculptures installed following their transfer from Wrest Park. Sir George Sitwell, on a visit to Jellicoe's office in 1937, had nonetheless claimed that the sculpture was too small in scale, an error common to most English design

CHAPTER 4
THE POLITICS OF LANDSCAPE

*'The values of the classical age have a profound bearing
on architecture today'*

*'Jellicoe saw the ways in which the human subconscious interpreted
feelings and how artists expressed these through their work'*

Broadway had shown Jellicoe that the *laissez-faire* world of free access and even freer environmental rights was on its way out. Although he was born while Queen Victoria was still on the throne and when the internal combustion engine was a futurist fantasy, by 1940 Jellicoe held no illusions about progress. At school when the old world was supposed to have died with the shots fired at Sarajevo, as a young architectural student he could be forgiven for embracing the balmy Indian summer of the 1920s and for pursuing a historical bent, even sharing with Jock Shepherd in a measure of inspired exploration. The Renaissance gardens of Italy had proved a spirited refuge for Shepherd after his war experiences;[1] for Jellicoe they were an academic exercise that might help to establish his own budding architectural credentials more firmly in an England that was unremittingly conservative and deeply imbued with a culture now redolent with nostalgia.

Just as teaching did not ultimately suit Shepherd, to Jellicoe it came as a vital opening. Through the Architectural Association he came in touch with the modern movement's early experiments. Even though Charles Rennie Mackintosh wasted away unknown in London, and the new experiments in design on the Continent were barely known in England, the student body itself was explorative, and a climate for new ideas gradually developed which surged to fulfilment at the AA

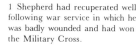

1 Shepherd had recuperated well following war service in which he was badly wounded and had won the Military Cross.

towards the end of the 1920s. Accordingly, by 1930 the old world had, at least at the AA, been supplanted by the modern. The key building of the Paimio Sanatorium by Alvar Aalto was already under construction in Finland; Le Corbusier's famous Villa Savoye was also being erected in France. For Jellicoe, the marvel of Cheddar Gorge influenced by Eric Mendelsohn was underway by 1935, and his modern commitment visible and unassailable. But it was to be an isolated opportunity, for all his efforts to develop a practice along such lines, and he was fortunate now to have a reputation in garden expertise which assured him of projects in this field. He could still feel in the centre of events, or close to them. When King Edward VIII, as he briefly was, took Wallis Simpson to meet the Yorks at Royal Lodge, the newly acquired American Buick station wagon also took them to view Jellicoe's innovations there. It was an age of illusion. The main achievement for Jellicoe was to have survived in architectural practice at all through a period of financial despondency.

As the end of the 1930s loomed, and the possibility of another war approached and then briefly receded, Jellicoe found himself drawn into a new controversy at the AA over teaching appointments. There had been a student rebellion, and it transpired that the only two acceptable figures for the post of Principal were Maxwell Fry and Jellicoe; Jellicoe applied and secured the post.[2] When war broke out one of his first tasks was to relocate the school out of London for the duration of hostilities. He took a car northwards towards Hertfordshire, announcing that he would not return until a new place had been found. Finding a pleasant house in Barnet, he knocked on the door, and the owners agreed to let it.

The Russell Page world, as Jellicoe refers to it, collapsed with the coming of war, and for a period Jellicoe divided his time between the remnants of his design office, the AA School (of which he was now Principal), and the skeleton Institute of Landscape Architects; to this was now added his service as an air raid warden. Still in his early forties, but beyond military age, Jellicoe found to his surprise that war work created new opportunities. With a staff that soon numbered over forty his office expanded dramatically. Charged with official responsibility for bomb repairs in the Islington area, he decided to put fees from that source directly towards the

2 Architectural Association Annual Records, 1939.

Hemel Hempstead, the Water Gardens, drawing by Geoffrey Jellicoe; see also pages 70-72

Geoffrey and Susan Jellicoe, c 1948

landscape profession; nonetheless, the Ministry of Supply soon charged him with several *housing* projects all over southern England.[3] In 1939 he had become President of the Institute of Landscape Architects, but the professional work was entirely on major programmes in building and planning and in providing essential emergency accommodation.

Throughout this period Jellicoe's administrative skills developed apace. The problem, however, was that the creativity of the artist inside could find no outlet. And the only consolation was that he began to foresee from experience how the post-war world of landscape would be very different from that of the pre-war.

An important opportunity to return to landscape practice occurred however, when on 8 October 1942 Geoffrey Jellicoe, together with other officials, visited the Hope Valley in the Peak District of Derbyshire. Jellicoe was asked to prepare a preliminary planning report.[4] In it, delivered to the Ministry of Town and Country Planning, he recommended 'that a landscape plan, in association with the industrial plan, be prepared for development over a number of years'. He followed this with a landscape plan for a period of fifty years or more. This project, optimistic in context at a time when the war could still have been lost, did more to provide Geoffrey Jellicoe with creative motivation than any other.

Hope Cement Works is one of Jellicoe's major landscapes, and one to which he has attached considerable importance. At the time of writing (1991) the half century nears its end, and the project is discussed in greater detail in the next chapter. Suffice it to say here that it brought Jellicoe face to face with the politics of landscape and the growing pressures of industrial growth, and led him directly to the realisation that in the post-war world his role would be to contain the social

3 Housing for UK Ministry of Supply: Theale, Berkshire; Hereford; Newport, Monmouthshire; Cardiff; Worcester; Poole, Dorset.
4 Preliminary Planning Report on the Hope Valley Project, 1943.

The home sanctuary — the garden at Grove Terrace in 1938

and economic threats poised by the new scales of operation. He realised that the designer's role extended not just to domestic surroundings; it extended now across the whole environment. It was a far cry from Ditchley.

In the war years, Jellicoe became adept at negotiating and working with official bodies, and in this respect he obtained experience that could never have been gained in peacetime professional practice. As the war closed, Jellicoe, at the prime of his life, was uniquely poised to take advantage of the new opportunities in planning and landscape architecture that the peace was to provide.

By 1946 the Jellicoes had occupied Grove Terrace for ten years. This home, and even more perhaps this garden, helped to preserve a sense of 'gardenscape', giving that vital link with seasonal change and plant growth. Cast like many at this time

Perspective of the original scheme for Hemel Hempstead. The Water Gardens can be seen stretching back centre left

into role upon role of dramatically increased responsibility, without it Jellicoe would have found it hard to nourish his sensibilities as a designer of landscape.

After the war Jellicoe undertook a range of new projects. While around the country post-war austerity saw to it that landscape projects were limited, garden work was non-existent. Only at the end of the 1940s did a touch of the old classicism return as a reminder of pre-war pleasures. Old clients had yet to reappear. In 1951, Ronald Tree, committed as ever, and true to form, commissioned Jellicoe to execute another Palladian celebration, Heron Bay, a mansion by the sea in white coral in Barbados. In the same year, Jellicoe dutifully executed another housing project in total contrast, the Lansbury Neighbourhood Housing Scheme in Poplar, East London.

He had naturally also hoped to gain the commission for the Battersea Gardens project at the 1951 Festival of Britain; he had few regrets, however, when the ubiquitous Russell Page secured it. In any event, as Jellicoe recalls:

> I had fallen out with the organiser, Gerald Barry, about a year or two before the Festival of Britain schemes were being prepared. The *News Chronicle* had organised a remarkable design modelled for the town of Knutsford...I was appointed landscape architect over the whole area. Barry, who as editor of the *News Chronicle* inspired this scheme (and, in fact, inspired the Festival of Britain proposals), while he liked my total scheme very much disagreed with me on one point. There was an area round the lake near the factories which I had kept pure green grass and the factory workers weren't allowed to go on this because I didn't want it spoilt. Now he said they ought to be able to use this area for lunchtime recreation and this was a significant moment in social history, because in a way he was quite right. But I said they would spoil it

View of the Hemel Hempstead Water Gardens, 1959

and I wouldn't budge, so because of that I lost the Battersea job. . .in this life you must every now and then stand on a principle and this was a principle I wasn't going to give way on.

It was undoubtedly a setback for Jellicoe that he was not involved in this major design. As J M Richards, former Editor of *The Architectural Review* (and on the Festival's Architecture Council) made clear, there was much scope for wholesale experimentation. The South Bank layout was:

> . . .a live experiment, devised by Casson and Mischa Black, in the adaptation of the English Picturesque tradition to urban instead of garden landscapes. . .The exhibition showed how the eighteenth century Picturesque devices, such as controlled irregularity and the disclosure one by one of unexpected elements in the landscape by exploiting a moving viewpoint can add a new dimension to the urban scene: a sense of liveliness, an invitation to personal participation.[5]

Jellicoe was, so to speak, working on parallel lines. The plan for Hemel Hempstead delivered one jewel to the inhabitants, which in the 1980s they were fighting desperately to save: Jellicoe's centrally disposed Water Gardens. Hemel Hempstead, as a New Town Corporation, like others of the time, was a composite body and in his negotiations Jellicoe drew many arguments. However, he

5 *Memoirs of an Unjust Fella,* Sir James Richards, Weidenfeld & Nicolson, 1980, p241.

Jellicoe designed the surface shape of the water for the Hemel Hempstead Water Gardens in the form of a serpent — the lake being the head and the canal the body. Compare this with the drawing on pages 66 and 67

University of Nottingham, model of the landscape plan showing the central area

managed to keep a good relationship. Other parts of Jellicoe's proposals for Hemel Hempstead were ultimately rejected, but with hindsight the unexecuted design he made for the centre of the new town has a linear grandeur and a totality of landscape environment that would find sympathy today if it had been built.

Jellicoe was also engaged on landscape plans for Nottingham University in 1955. This precursor to much of the university planning of the 1960s and 1970s was highly praised: cars were suppressed, and the human scale maintained and enhanced by means of gardens and groves of trees; an amphitheatre (a favourite Jellicoe ploy) was appended to an existing lake; an evident park-like character was sustained which could otherwise have been fragmented and lost; and a strict ceiling level was placed upon the capacity of the site to take further proposed building.

Discernible in Jellicoe's work of the 1950s, especially at Hemel Hempstead, is a growing interest in deeper preoccupations in landscape and the environment. Despite the heavy involvement in planning committees, and the consequent need to reconcile not only purely environmental concerns but also essentially political considerations, Jellicoe developed the habit of dissimulating, withdrawing to home ground, to the recesses of the garden at Grove Terrace, to explore these deeper preoccupations and, as he described it at the time, to 'grope' towards the essential grains of a philosophy.

In the late 1950s, while Susan Jellicoe worked on the planting plans for Hemel Hempstead (establishing a mutual working pattern that lasted until the 1980s at Sutton Place), Geoffrey was putting the finishing touches to *Studies in Landscape*

Giovanni Bellini, 'The Earthly Paradise' (c 1480-90), Uffizi, Florence. Jellicoe claims that for him this is the most moving of all landscape paintings: 'Such organisation of space (as opposed to evocation of space) is the ambition . . . of every landscape architect'. The picture exemplifies the final stage in Bellini's progress from using landscape as backcloth or architectural frame to pure landscape: 'Rocks, distant building and nature in tranquillity'. In the first volume of Studies in Landscape Design *Jellicoe indicates four specific characteristics of the painting as a means to clarifying their relevance to contemporary landscape design:*
1. The floor pattern is not only beautiful in itself; it is related to, and draws into the foreground (by colour as well as form) the interspersed buildings in the distance.
2. The balustrade interlocks foreground and middle distance.
3. The Madonna's throne, the only rich element of architectural detail, links the human figures to the geometric foreground.
4. We then realise that the foreground figures are too small in scale for the balustrade, which is severely plain and nearly four feet in height; whereas in the background the distant figures are well over life size. Note the two-foot-high fence near the cross, and how the figure in the cave is unduly cramped. The distant standing couple is almost heroic.

Design. In this first volume of three, published in 1960, he drew together history and contemporary work in England. He emphasised, however, that the studies were concerned only with ideas. The overall perspective was international; the scope, to borrow from Gropius, was 'total'; the ideas were wholly contemporary.

Furthermore there was one unique thread of observation that ran through the book like quicksilver: the close connection of landscape with art, a realisation which in Jellicoe had been germinating since his studies of Italian Renaissance gardens. In the first volume of *Studies* it surfaced in an articulate formulation for the first time through the example of the works of Perugino, Botticelli, Bellini, Tintoretto, Giorgione and Cézanne, as well as through contemporary works, the favoured artists being John Nash, Graham Sutherland, Ivon Hitchens, Ben Nicholson, Henry Moore and Victor Pasmore. Significantly a work by Paul Klee appears in this context for the first time.

Tintoretto, 'Susannah and the Elders' (c 1560), Kunsthistorisches Museum, Vienna. Jellicoe charts the change in painterly concepts about landscape space by comparing this painting with the Bellini, and by means of the accompanying diagram describes the basic landscape format upon which Tintoretto relied. Jellicoe also analyses how such space can be manipulated by using patterns of screens that are related to each other by abstract design rather than by geometry:

1. The heart of the composition is the union of Susannah and the green screen. The one is in every way a foil to the other, in form, light, texture, and purpose; and how beautifully they are united by towel, ornaments and mirror.

2. Susannah is supported and stabilised by her tree, and thereafter the spaces flow round the screens. It is these screens that are of intense interest, because without them the spaces would lose their significance and not be spaces at all.

3. The eye of the beholder is invited to pass easily over obstructions across the path and so out of the picture, whereas the physical body cannot easily do the same.

4. In the painting there are two scales: that crossing the foreground, and that of the distance, the two being linked by the screen. In reality there is no play upon change of scale, as in the 'Allegory'; the second Elder, for instance, being harmonious with the caryatid, which properly tends to be heroic. The difference is one of perspective only.

5. There is intense interest from incidents based on the most minute perception, supplied as it were free of charge as a gift from nature.

Where gardens were concerned, a few designers had embraced the spirit of contemporary art before the war, in much the same way as the picturesque movement had drawn its perspectives from the paintings of Poussin and Claude. *The Studio,* for example, had published a Special Winter Number at the end of 1926 on the subject of 'modern gardens'.[6] This barometer of taste had thus travelled a remarkable way since the pedestrian surveys edited by Charles Holme in the 1900s. Appreciation of contemporary garden design had certainly lagged well behind that in the applied arts as they followed the modern direction.

Earlier coverage by *The Studio* had left much to be desired, but by 1926, however, stalwart efforts were being made to rectify the depressed situation. The general malaise had restricted the scope of such journals as *Country Life* where the clock had stuck with Lutyens.

6 'Modern Gardens, British and Foreign', *The Studio,* Special Winter Number, 1926, text Percy Cane; includes work by Peter Behrens, Tony Garnier, Oliver Hill, Josef Hoffmann, M H Baillie-Scott, Avray Tipping.

Paul Cézanne, 'Lac d'Annecy'. The degree to which Cézanne simplified natural forms — leaves, grass, mountains, reveals for Jellicoe his insight about the essential structure of the environment. Cézanne used wide variations of colour in light to convey differing forms of landscape element

John Nash, 'Cros de Cagnes', 1927. Nash had a special ability to reflect the inner 'subconscious' meaning of a given landscape without embellishment or subterfuge. Unlike his brother Paul, who encouraged him to paint, John Nash had no formal training

Ivon Hitchens, 'Sea of Bracken'. Hitchens' work particularly appeals to Jellicoe for its skill in capturing the elusive essence of landscape, both in its structure and in its spatial recession. Using the minimum deployment of paint, and by virtually eliminating botanical detail and formal structure, he succeeds in portraying the mysteries of landscape form both as remembered and as fully perpetrated in the subconscious mind of man

Victor Pasmore, untitled. In Pasmore's work Jellicoe admires the way the artist has moved gradually towards abstraction of form, forsaking the seductive riverside views of his early career for an idiom that gives fuller scope to the workings of his subconscious and its yearnings for a freer natural form

Paul Klee, 'Highways and Byways', 1929. Of all contemporary artists, the Swiss artist Paul Klee has undoubtedly had the greatest influence upon Geoffrey Jellicoe. Although almost a generation older than Jellicoe, Klee provided Jellicoe with a wide range of inspiration, not only through his work, but also by virtue of his method. Although the two artists never met, Jellicoe has felt drawn to Klee's example over many decades, and has said of Klee that he 'pierced the instinct transparencies almost to their lowest depth and [had] drawn upon his own peculiar mix.'

Richard Sudell had led the formation of the British Association of Garden Architects in 1927, which in due course re-emerged in 1929, with the support of both Oliver Hill and Geoffrey Jellicoe, as the Institute of Landscape Architects. But an awareness of the modern, and its relationship with art, architecture and landscape was mournfully slow in emerging even in informed English circles.[7] The spirit was elusive: only Christopher Tunnard in his designs for Bentley Wood grasped contemporary meaning by inserting a Henry Moore sculpture (now removed) at a crucial point.[8]

Jellicoe's post-war involvement with contemporary art developed in the 1950s through his contacts with artists and one other architect, Frederick Gibberd

7 See Geoffrey Jellicoe's series of articles 'The Theoretical Planning of Gardens', *Architects Journal*, 11 November 1931, p640; 9 December 1931, p776; 6 January 1932, p16; 3 February 1932, p186; 2 May 1932, p318; 6 April 1932, p472.
8 Tunnard's key work, *Gardens in the Modern Landscape*, collating a 1938 series of his *Architectural Review* articles, did not appear until 1939.

(planner of Harlow New Town and already a keen collector of contemporary painting and sculpture). The difference from Tunnard was that Jellicoe saw the ways in which the human subconscious interpreted feelings and how artists expressed these through their work. If artists could carry a message and relevance for modern society, striking an echo, Jellicoe reasoned, could these sentiments not equally well be touched by man's involvement with the landscape?

Historically artists such as Claude, Poussin and Wilson had demonstrated a way of looking at the natural landscape with which man is always involved, and this attitude had a contemporary yet still picturesque corollary in the work of certain contemporary garden designs, such as those by Rob Mallet-Stevens, Gabriel Guevrekian[9] and Tunnard.

But Jellicoe was reaching for something much more profound than the creation of modernistic 'model' views that simply replicated the picturesque tradition, or else pursued abstract ideas.

As yet, immersed in the busy activity of both architectural and landscape practice, Jellicoe had found little time or opportunity to test out his ideas. And generally it must be said that few architects themselves had any better understanding of the importance of art, indeed architecture was wholly divorced from painting and sculpture in Britain. For those with a sense of history, like Christopher Hussey, this was deeply to be regretted. For his friend Geoffrey Jellicoe, came the realisation that in landscape, as in historical gardens, art might be the key to unlock a deeper understanding.

As the 1960s progressed, Geoffrey Jellicoe's practice built up to cover an increasingly wide range of projects. While there were fewer gardens to design, he was increasingly in demand where towns and cities came under increased pressure from traffic expansion. A series of schemes was commissioned by English cities, Gloucester, Oxford and Cheltenham, and environmental design recommendations were required by the Scilly Isles and later by the Isle of Sark.

Geoffrey Jellicoe reported on Gloucester in December 1961. The city was

9 Gabriel Guevrekian had worked in Vienna with Josef Hoffmann, but on settling in Paris worked in Mallet-Stevens' office and contributed his own cubist garden design for the 1925 Paris Exposition des Arts Décoratifs. Mallet-Stevens himself contributed a more traditional design. Guevrekian's was recognised to be the first serious effort to raise garden design to the intellectual level of modern painting.

becoming choked with cars and, more particularly, the cathedral was hemmed in by car parks and hence virtually isolated from the city to which it gave such a clear historic and visual identity. From afar, Jellicoe argued, here was a remarkable landmark:

> Under certain conditions of light there is perhaps no other view of landscape so truly English as that of the Severn valley when seen from the Cotswolds. From this vantage point it is clear that the Cathedral tower still dominates the scene, and this dominance can be retained in perpetuity without at the same time frustrating future development.[10]

Characteristically, Jellicoe proposed a direct solution, yet one which was a convincing articulation of the deep structure of the historic grain of Gloucester. He conceived of a major and extensive pedestrian route (the 'Via Sacra') between 'church' and 'gown' linking all parts of the ancient city and opening a traditional view of the cathedral (see overleaf). From the cathedral the route links up with the ancient St Mary de Lode, possibly the first Christian church in England, via the Greyfriars and Blackfriars buildings. 'A single majestic idea' is how Jellicoe described the rediscovery of the city's ancient identity by means of the Via Sacra.

Recalled in 1966, Geoffrey Jellicoe defined a Height of Buildings Policy to preserve the primary silhouette of the city. Unlike the shriller conservationists of the 1980s, Jellicoe maintained that historic silhouette and modern silhouette could coexist, providing that the juxtaposition of the latter is carefully controlled.

Oxford City Council approached Jellicoe in 1963 to help them find a solution to the vexed problem of taking a traffic relief road across Christ Church Meadow. This, like Gloucester, was an extremely sensitive area. Clearly a tunnel was economically out of the question and Jellicoe proposed another typically forthright solution: a sunken road that relied upon visual illusion (an old landscape trick) to conceal reality from the naked eye. The river was to be diverted and the whole of the road was to be sunk some seventeen and a half feet.

Questioned by the press, Jellicoe argued that the best solution was to make the road seem to disappear. He had called on the arts of illusion in the landscape.

It was natural for an architect to want to make his mark on Oxford:

> But I like to think that one's mark on Oxford will be that there is no mark at all...I think the expenditure would be entirely justified. One has the feeling that this meadow is primitive and reaches down to one's deepest feelings.

The primitive roughness of the meadow Jellicoe saw as a method of confusing the eye of the observer, and he referred to the ethos of Humphry Repton, whom he quoted:

> Deception may be allowable in imitating the works of nature; thus artificial rivers, lakes and rock scenery can only be great by deception, and the mind acquiesces in the fraud, after it is detected; but in works of art every trick ought to be avoided. Sham churches, sham rivers, sham bridges, and everything which appears what it is not, disgusts when the trick is discovered.[11]

10 *A Comprehensive Plan for the Central Area of the City of Gloucester*, December 1961.
11 *The Landscape Gardening and Landscape Architecture of the Late Humphry Repton Esq*, J C Loudon, Longman & Co, 1840, p163, statement dated 1802.

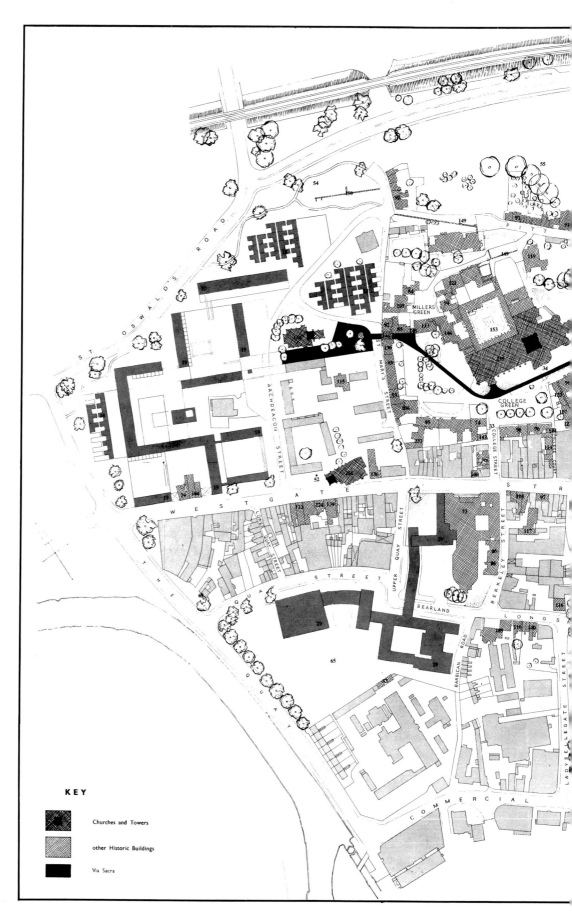

The City of Gloucester: the Via Sacra is shown by the black line

KEY

Churches and Towers

other Historic Buildings

Via Sacra

80

Oxford from the air. Christ Church Meadow is centre right

Jellicoe's interest in the meadow derived from a much deeper awareness of the significance of this open space opposite Christ Church than its face value would suggest; he had done his research fastidiously. He discovered that the Dean of Christ Church in the mid-nineteenth century, Dean Liddell, had taken an essentially pragmatic view of the meadow: its function was to provide a restfulness of mind and to allow access to boats on the Cherwell. By creating 'long low lines of grassland, its occasional groups of trees giving shade to cattle, and the grazing cattle themselves, it must have had some affinity with the art of Théodore Rousseau'. As Kenneth Clark has commented, Rousseau's response to nature was to the static rather than the dynamic...'his most genuine emotions were aroused by the absolute stillness of a summer day'.[12] Jellicoe decided that this creation of stillness was the main objective of Liddell when he closed the meadow to river scenery, for in Dean Liddell's time the railways had arrived, peace had been shattered, and stillness had to be regained. Furthermore this concept of a meadow, in such a context, was of special interest and importance:

> It is an affair of the mind rather than the eye; the eye conveys what it sees,
> but it is the mind that turns the image into a vast world of the imagination.[13]

In fact, such was the value of the meadow in its existing form that, and possibly even as a result of Jellicoe's appraisal, it remained unchanged.

Geoffrey Jellicoe was soon afterwards invited to prepare a scheme of considerable importance to the city of Cheltenham, when he was asked to design the new civic baths and amphitheatre on an adjoining site to Pittville — an important spa building, designed in 1827. The site lay beyond a series of lakes, carefully set in a nineteenth century visual paradigm of Elysian fields; the 'Fairy Lake' as it was known locally when created in the nineteenth century.

Jellicoe was faced here with two alternative strategies: he could create, as he said, 'a classical-romantic landscape where the building dominates skyline and scenery, or a romantic-classical landscape in which the buildings become subsidiary'. He went for the latter and, furthermore, had the idea of reversing landscape elements: the valley to become a hill, the implied flow of the spring

12 *Landscape into Art,* Kenneth Clark, John Murray, 1949, p80.
13 *Studies in Landscape Design,* Vol II, Geoffrey Jellicoe, OUP, 1966, p65.

Théodore Rousseau (1812-67), 'A Summer Day', Louvre

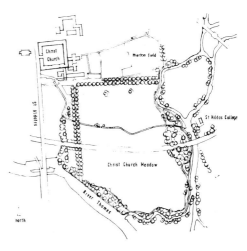

Plan of Christ Church Meadow showing the proposed altered course of the Cherwell

waters to be turned to flow 'out of the hill, as a good spring should'. He established a thick screen of trees, to draw the landscape away from the building, relating it to the outline of the original valley, and he created a viewpoint from the new hill allowing a panorama of both the surrounding Cotswold hills and, in the distance, the Malvern hills. A railway, hitherto a dominant indication of nineteenth century progress on the site, was 'converted' visually into a tree-lined road (the Way), and rendered less obtrusive; and the mound, a characteristic Jellicoe element, was skilfully inserted to link these disparate constructs together. The new hill was planted with trees and would thus continue to grow over a generation or so. Jellicoe named it, appropriately, Mount Kronos. The relationship of amphitheatre to surrounding landscape is one of harmony between building and distant perspective; essentially Grecian, the scheme draws its inspiration from Delphi.

Describing the scheme later in *Studies in Landscape Design* Jellicoe explains how

Model of Delphi. Jellicoe was influenced by Delphi in his plan for the Cheltenham scheme

83

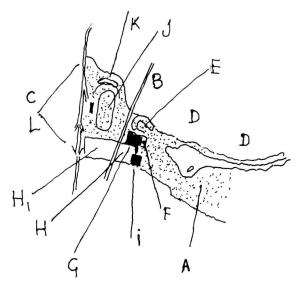

Existing landscape	Executed works	Projected works
A Pittville park and lake	E Open-air theatre	H₁ Car park
B Road	F Sculpture garden	I Sports pavilion
C Railway on embankment	G Swimming pool	J Stadium
D Golf course	complex	K Mount Kronos
	H Car park	L Road replacing
		railway

Cheltenham was really a case study, from his point of view, into the interaction of the past with the modern. In the late 1960s, it must be remembered, the modernist standpoint was a reaction to an excess of academic construction in architecture which had rendered advances in building technology of the first quarter-century virtually useless. Jellicoe had lived through this period as a student. Now that he saw more clearly the continued relevance of classicism (as had Picasso and Le Corbusier) he used as examples Picasso's recreations of the classical scene in the 'Vollard Suite', and quoted Le Corbusier on the Acropolis, although he was at pains to indicate the contrast between the Acropolis and Delphi where buildings do not dominate the landscape but are subsidiary to it.

However, to Jellicoe, this lesson from history did not demand a corresponding architectural elucidation in the form of a building replicating the details of the classical age. His point was that the *values* of that age have a profound bearing upon architecture today. Architecturally, Jellicoe's contemporary design sits elegantly and readily within the Cheltenham urban picturesque, as remodelled, but does not dominate it; it is the open-air theatre that forms the terminus to the sequence of lakes, and not the baths complex. As at Delphi, it is the Way which links the diversity of the landscaped site together and which communicates those values, that meaning.

In 1965, the developing field of environmental planning claimed Geoffrey Jellicoe's attention in a remarkable way: he was commissioned to prepare a landscape plan for the Isles of Scilly, a project which occupied him for a full year. As with his pioneering plan for Broadway, over thirty years earlier, this was essentially a conservation study. He proposed what he then called a 'Charter for the Isles of Scilly':

> One had to relate a very tremendous piece of natural landscape to the doings of man and man of course does change with the times. It wasn't preservation; it was more conservation. How to sustain the ethos of the islands without it being destroyed by speculators, and the major thing, which has been very difficult indeed, was to restrict the population coming in so that you only have a limited number of people using the islands at all.[14]

14 Ibid, Vol III, 1970, pp38, 39.

This particular garden of the mind bore all the hallmarks of the lessons learnt over

Cheltenham: model of the sports centre, baths and open-air theatre

a span of forty years; but it was also mindful of the realities of the late twentieth century explosion of tourism, the quantitative constraints of which had only been touched upon in the Broadway plan. As with Broadway, the community concerned remained in consultation with him and sought his seal on their continued adherence to his established principles as late as 1985.

The Isle of Sark forms a part of the Channel Islands and, unlike the Scillies, the islands tend towards a more pronounced individuality. In 1967 Geoffrey Jellicoe was called in by the local authority (the Chief Pleas) with the unanimous support of the Dame of Sark (the traditional ruler) and the local Amenities Committee, to prepare a landscape plan for the island. To Jellicoe, Sark is a microcosm of a world problem. He saw the challenge as one for resolving the way in which a small, remote community can come to terms with the pressures of the modern world, and he felt that a successful solution might, in principle, be applicable on a wider scale:

> Can the landscape of the island project itself into the modern world as a continuity of history? Or are the external pressures so great that it must break with history, and become a scene of indiscriminate building, shanties, and wirescape which express all the uncertain values of the present age?

What had initially been considered a demographic necessity now became the key to the successful implementation of his report — the restriction of population. Jellicoe did not however propose birth control, but control by restriction of further growth through natural regeneration and rising standards of space for the present islanders (half of whom, at the time, were already classified as incomers). Jellicoe in his plan recognised that the homes were mostly grouped in clusters, heavily planted 'clumps', each house having rights of access to the sea. The distribution pattern of trees he considered to be a vital historical characteristic of the place: none grew below the one hundred foot contour, and those evidently were confined to roads or small plantations around the clusters of houses.

Sark was, of course, both an ecology (including humans) and a landscape of shelters. In spring or summer, all might seem a garden, but in autumn and winter the exposed conditions could render it more a desolate but inhabited rock. To cross the high and exposed link between Great and Little Sark was to realise a perilous nature in the communications route that Turner was at pains to depict so

Jellicoe's proposed plan for Sark recognised the traditional landscape of the clusters of dwellings, each set compactly among its fields

Aerial view of Sark

J M W Turner, 'La Coupée'. Turner's painting illustrates the dramatic effect on travellers when crossing from Great to Little Sark

dramatically, even going so far as to exaggerate the drama, but not perhaps the effect, on the traveller crossing the land bridge, La Coupée.

Jellicoe's proposals were most specific: tree-planting along roads or in groups, reinforcing the clusters of dwellings, together with an essential and characteristic Jellicoe concept, that of a footpath around Little Sark linked to a coastal system of paths around Great Sark. Other considerations related to the control of 'wirescape' and the restoration of the hereditary landscape with its buildings.

But a year later he was chastened to find his proposals ultimately rejected by fifteen votes to twelve, only half of the council committee members being present. It was a salutary lesson in the realities of democratic town planning, albeit on a tiny scale. Jellicoe felt that his proposals had unearthed deeply possessive instincts, compounded by a misunderstanding of his relatively simple proposals as 'interference with existing laws and hence with the machinery of nature'. He consoled himself on the flight back to England with readings from Robert Ardrey's *The Territorial Imperative,* [15] published while the Sark study was in progress. Subtitled 'A Personal Inquiry into the Animal Origins of Property and Nations', it reminded him that 'a territory is an area of space which an animal or group of animals defends as an exclusive preserve'. Ardrey had taken a concept well understood by biologists and argued that man obeyed the same laws. If Sark was a microcosm, it seemed from his experience all the more a fact.

In 1965 Jellicoe had a further taste of the politics of post-war environmental planning, when he was commissioned by the City Corporation of Edinburgh to prepare a plan for the Tollcross area of Edinburgh.[16] At the core of this area lay an existing shopping centre which, although viable, was in need of modernisation. The whole area apparently lacked planning cohesion, and landscaping as such was

15 *The Territorial Imperative,* Robert Ardrey, London, 1967.
16 Tollcross Area of Edinburgh Plan, February 1965.

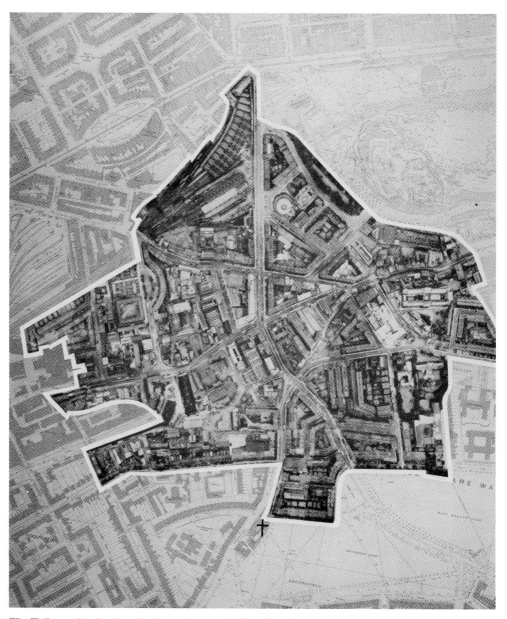

The Tollcross site. Lothian Road runs in a straight line down the centre of the shaded area; Barclay Church is indicated by a cross

virtually non-existent. However, Jellicoe recognised one important urban axis — the length of Lothian Road on to the historically notable Barclay Church. In civic design terms he described the rest as a 'civic jungle', the housing was substandard and areas were already blighted. There were major areas of potential, however, and the possibility of a 'festival area' as an all-the-year-round nucleus of activity for the Edinburgh International Festival, subsequently to be realised in the late 1980s as Festival Square and environs.

The conjunction of the inner ring road, Lothian Road, West Port and Lauriston Place was articulated by an egg-shaped ring: two webs, one for traffic, a second for pedestrians, were gently laid over a new matrix of formalised landscape areas or 'cells', and the west pavement of Lothian Road was totally reconstructed to create a tree-lined boulevard enhancing major commerical frontages. This formed

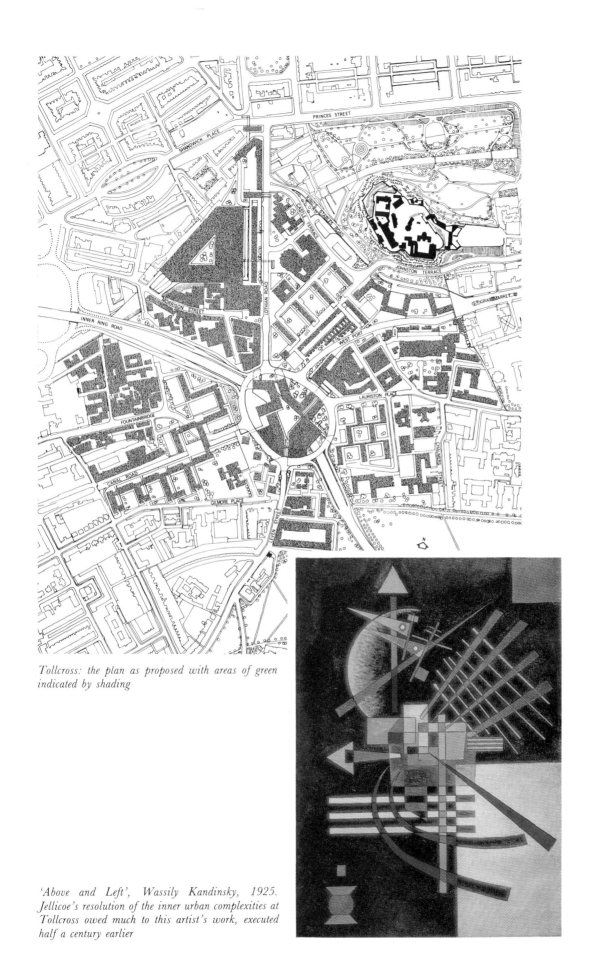

Tollcross: the plan as proposed with areas of green indicated by shading

'Above and Left', Wassily Kandinsky, 1925. Jellicoe's resolution of the inner urban complexities at Tollcross owed much to this artist's work, executed half a century earlier

the principle pedestrian axis in a wholly independent system of pedestrian circulation. Jellicoe found inspiration here in the work of Kandinsky with its dynamic correlation of conflicting forms. The centre of the 'egg' was filled with a modernised shopping centre drawing in existing stores. The concept overall was bold and, while respecting the nineteenth century scale of Edinburgh, it infused this with a flexible urban structure. The newly proposed festival area sought to create a lively piazza, not just a setting down area, outside the Usher Hall, the kind of space that exists inside major cities such as Vienna and Prague.

While these key projects occupied the Jellicoe office for more than a decade, there were certain other schemes received and delivered that maintained what had always been, *inter alia,* an architect's practice.

Following his design for contemporary buildings at Mablethorpe, on the North Sea coast of Lincolnshire, a project which emerged in 1946 as an absolutely clear exposition of functionalism with elegance, Jellicoe stood unequivocally in line with his 1930s' AA students (many of them like Anthony and Oliver Cox and Denys Lasdun now emerging as successful post-war practitioners), and a series of well-articulated public buildings link Cheddar Gorge through to the 1970s.

While Cheltenham was predominantly landscape over building, the crematorium building at Grantham (1966) reverses this relationship, as if the sombre function it contains and its human implications need a spiritual boost, man over nature. On a slightly elevated site on the outskirts of the city, yet within site of its historic spires, Jellicoe concentrated his message within the symbolism of the free-standing cross and the spire and circle it contains (in fact a chimney with essential smoke vent). The building is utterly without decoration, with some of the mood of a departure terminal in a private aviation concern, and only the chimney and the cross remind us of the building's particular purpose. It is in the landscape potential of the informal and contemplative garden of remembrance that faces the simple crucifix that the mind and spirit can be restored from grief and hopelessness.

Towards the end of the 1960s, Jellicoe had executed the design for a major hotel project in Lusaka (the capital of Northern Rhodesia, now Zambia) and a building which is one of the city's best-preserved landmarks; once again the solution was uncompromisingly contemporary, and somewhat ahead of its time, certainly in the African continent.

Following completion of this, essentially a new building-type for Geoffrey Jellicoe but one with considerable environmental potential as the tourist industry began to expand worldwide, he had high hopes of opportunities to work again combining large building projects with surrounding landscape. But this was not to be. It may be that in the complex professional world of the post-war period, and with an established practice spanning town and country planning, architecture, landscaping and gardens, he had spread his net widely but rather too thinly. With excellent supporting partners and staff, and a particularly high standard of quality control in design, there was, however, a limit to the availability of architectural work — though there seemed to be no limit, in terms of professional criteria and quality, as to what Jellicoe could offer.

Model of the Mablethorpe project

Grantham Crematorium. The spire-chimney is on the left

Layout showing the relationship of the Grantham Crematorium (top) with the nineteenth century cemetery (below). The cross dominates the landscape and links the two areas

In 1963 (with Hal Moggridge as his assistant) Jellicoe produced a unique visionary project to bridge the Thames in London. It caused a buzz of excitement through both the architectural profession itself and the broader public and caught the imagination of a generation in search of a new dimension in architecture; it had impeccable historical antecedents (as always with Jellicoe); it was remarkably prescient of built structures to emerge in the following fifteen years from North America to Japan; and it was viable in economic terms. Crystal Span was the sixth project of a research group set up in the late 1950s by Pilkington Brothers, the glass industry giant, to explore in an imaginative way the architectural possibilities of glass as a building material. As sited at Vauxhall, Crystal Span superbly complemented the Tate Gallery, the nearby Millbank tower on the north bank,

Ridgway Hotel, Lusaka

Perspective of the Church Hill Memorial Garden, Walsall

and the new office complexes on the south of the river. It also fitted in with the existing pattern of bridges. Unlike other projects by the Glass Age Development Committee, it was entirely a Jellicoe concept. As the Ponte Vecchio was to the Uffizi in Florence, Crystal Span would be to the Tate Gallery, drawing both banks of the river together in a London analogy.

The transparent superstructure of the bridge consisted of a glass curtain, within which a pair of double-decked pre-stressed concrete box sections were suspended from cables running to the top of the concrete towers at four points along the bridge. Ove Arup and partners had evolved an economical structure where the box sections had solid side walls at the points of support, and open areas where the stresses were correspondingly lower.

As well as providing two decks of six-lane roadway and supporting ramps and access ways, the bridge also consisted of a 120-room hotel, roof gardens, an open-air theatre, a skating rink, shops over the roadways, exhibition halls, and ample parking space. The total cost was estimated in 1963 at some seven million pounds. The brief from Pilkington was for a structure envisaged fifty years ahead, but one that could be built now using contemporary materials. All things considered, the project design cannot be said in 1991 to have acquired any obsolescence, and seems even more relevant today. The project, as Jellicoe might say, is still on the table.

If the spread of Jellicoe's professional involvement was diffuse, and extended across the widening range of architectural expertise, albeit with something of a bias

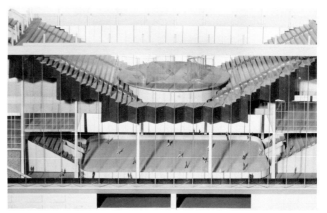

Left: Model of the Crystal Span. Right: The open-air theatre located within the superstructure of Crystal Span

Church Hill Memorial Garden: view of the gardens and one of the 'empty' gateways

towards environmental planning, it nonetheless continued to include, as a vital footing to his work in landscape, a number of garden design projects whereby he continued to develop the essential principles of design which would, in due course, come to a full flowering.

One of these designs, the Church Hill Memorial Garden in Walsall was commissioned as early as 1947. Essentially a war memorial to the fallen of the two World Wars it was early on defined as a memorial landscape and filled a sensitive area surrounding a fine church on elevated ground. The context was utterly traditional. The first part of the scheme comprised a new walled formal garden and viewing terrace; the second part involved the design of a close, protected from the south by a block of flats. An ecclesiastical building would, eventually, terminate the close. Jellicoe's proposals could, in the 1950s, have been termed historicist, yet they have caught the sense of a past tradition enshrined within the idea of a timeless memorial. The gateways to the walled garden are hollow porticoes complete with empty pediments which seem wholly appropriate in a contemporary post-modern sense. There is a strong vein of symbolism. Today, almost forty years later, the gardens are lush with growth, the walls and masonry well patinated. Gestures to the past abound but the landscape is of now.

Model of the Hope Cement Works; inset shows Geoffrey Jellicoe on the right, 1943

CHAPTER 5
THE LANDSCAPES OF MAN

'Jellicoe seeks to preserve the continuum of history, allowing for future amendment where appropriate to the overall tapestry of landscape history now clarified and preserved'

'An art form has neither beginning nor end, and the art itself is in the making and not the completion'

The English landscape has always been close to the heart of Geoffrey Jellicoe. At Broadway in 1933 he made his first proposals for the safeguarding of one highly valued part of the cultivated landscape, at the same time establishing recommendations that were intended to last for the foreseeable future. In the depths of war he was called to the Derbyshire Peak District, again through enlightened foresight, this time on the part of Sir George Earle. Earle's Cement Works, as it was originally called, lie opposite Win Hill, a prominent feature in the Hope Valley, in the centre of the Peak District. In 1943 a planned development schedule for the quarrying running for over half a century was presented by Jellicoe in the form of a phased model. As he wrote:

> The attack on the hills in such an historic position seems an attack on the very body of England, which indeed it is, and the arts of illusion have been used to recreate the hillside by waste material and thus reduce the apparent breach in the hill.

Returning as requested in October 1978, Jellicoe was commissioned to make a reassessment of the extent to which the 1943 plan had been followed through. He found that although the works had outgrown the finite classical scheme he had originally proposed, they had transformed themselves (through a demand higher than anticipated) into a new organic form that still kept to the principles of curtailment of silhouette. He realised that here was an art form of peculiar interest. It seemed as though the works developed an internal rhythm and that the duty of the independent landscape architect was to act as keeper to a monster whose growth was still wholly unforeseeable. In 1988 Jellicoe approved of yet another stage of growth. Of the project he says:

> It is the only work of landscape with which I have been associated that fully upholds the diction of the American philosopher John Dewey that an art form has neither beginning nor end, and the art itself is in the making and not the completion.

The tree planting throughout has been consistent. Norway maple, poplar, ash and mountain ash are now rising tall and with variegated splendour amidst a ground cover of shrubs — dogwood, snowberry, guelder rose and wild privet. Older trees that were already established have been nurtured amidst the new plantations. The lakes seem to lie in naturally, fringed with birch and willow, closely wooded on their northern shores; and now natural regeneration is developing and extending what man began, while the ecology again welcomes considerable bird life.

Today, the ethos of the plan seems more than ever viable: in the late twentieth century heyday of unrestrained market economics, with their unpredictable propensity to change, Jellicoe's original guidelines have held and proved adaptable to the explosion of extractive activity that has occurred — one lake has not even approached the planned size, but others have been spawned as the project proceeds.

On his return to the Hope Cement Works in 1978, Jellicoe looked once again to art for a paradigm of the process which created the dynamic form. He found it in the work of the American abstract expressionists of the 1950s, and a forceful work by Jackson Pollock, 'Summertime', contains the echo to which Jellicoe could himself respond with a new confidence in man as well as with a degree of humility. The creative process was no longer a finite activity, the spectator no longer detached, and the work of art was all around, action-landscape as art.

In 1960, two remarkable yet distinctive landscape projects arrived in Jellicoe's office. Both had awesome aspects and, curiously, both were concerned with forces greater than man.

At Harwell, the Rutherford Laboratory was a project considered to be of national importance, and yet its impact on the surrounding soft Berkshire countryside and the nearby downs threatened to be severe in the extreme. At Oldbury, close to the Severn, the forces to be contained by the nuclear power station were no less potentially cataclysmic. Suddenly the playful optimism of the 1950s and the culture that stemmed from the Festival of Britain mood seemed muted in the Jellicoe office. Here were projects designed to assimilate forces of a literally inexplicable dimension that had to be reconciled with the timeless values of the English countryside. The Hope Valley programme, despite its relentless but slow growth, seemed suddenly conciliatory, at one with nature, when compared with Harwell and Oldbury.

Jellicoe had known and admired Henry Moore since the 1920s and Ben Nicholson was a close friend. In these two artists Jellicoe had noticed an absorption with the changes occurring in the twentieth century, and understood their attempts, together with those of the sculptor Barbara Hepworth, to come to terms with the natural world as they perceived it. After all, Jellicoe had, as an architect in the early 1930s with the Cheddar Gorge project, demonstrated his contemporary awareness in parallel with their work of the time as sculptors and painter.

Generally, the early 1960s can now be seen to have been a period of rapid transition; a time of considerable idealism accompanied by a wariness about the prospects for peaceful progress. Political leaders in West and East were suddenly again aware of the fragility of nuclear peace. Although Jellicoe was thinking of an

Hope Cement Works landscape development, as projected to 1993, drawn by Geoffrey Jellicoe in 1979. The quarries are shown in yellow. Disused quarries are fishing lakes with replanting to the north

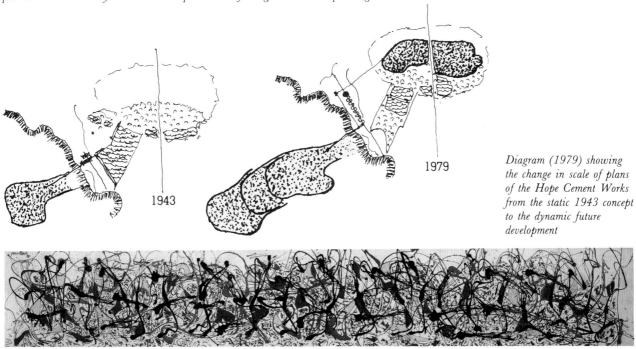

1943

1979

Diagram (1979) showing the change in scale of plans of the Hope Cement Works from the static 1943 concept to the dynamic future development

The dynamic expressed in painting: 'Summertime' by Jackson Pollock

Geoffrey Jellicoe and Ben Nicholson, c 1975. Nicholson was a close friend and his work an influence on Jellicoe's ideas on landscape design

Henry Moore, 'Draped Reclining Figure', 1952-3. In this work Jellicoe understood Moore's familiar motive which harks back to classical Greece in its naturalistic composition

earlier, more harmonious period in Moore's work, it is interesting that at this time Moore himself was entering a more sombre mood in sculpture. Herbert Read describes it thus:

> The last piece to be completed by Moore [in 1964] is the Atom Piece...
> The whole concept suggests the containment of a powerful force in the way
> that a compact skull holds a brain capable of the wildest fantasies. The Atom
> Piece symbolises those forces which modern man has released for ends which
> cannot be imagined or realised, but which for the present we inevitably
> associate with universal destruction. At the same time it negates this evil

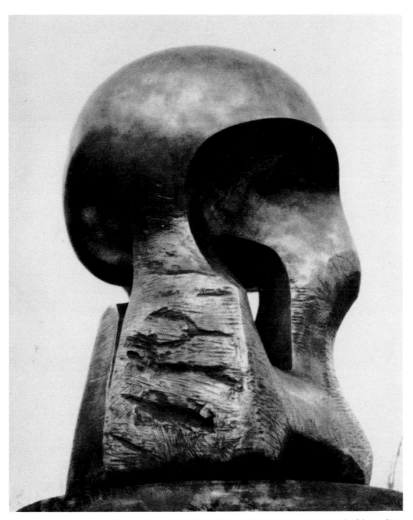

Henry Moore, 'Atom Piece', 1964. In the mid-1960s Henry Moore came to terms in his sculpture with the ominous threat of nuclear power. 'Atom Piece' is a large and haunting sculpture that sits menacingly in the landscape. Jellicoe at Harwell expressed the same reservations in his landscape about the forces 'which modern man has released for ends which cannot yet be imagined or realised'

intention and returns the contemplating mind to a mood of stillness and serenity.[1]

Jellicoe was profoundly aware of these forces and their implications, and at Harwell, therefore, he could not but produce a scheme that reflected these preoccupations. As he said:

> In the subterranean laboratories at the foot of the hills the most advanced scientific studies as yet made by man are taking place. The scientist himself will tell you that the splitting of the atom leads to infinity, or as one scientist put it 'to God'. The mathematical sciences have far outstripped the biological sciences, and this disequilibrium, as we all know, could lead to the eventual destruction of the human race. Opposed to this fearful intellectual development is the human body that is still the same as ever, and within this body but very deep down under layers of civilisation, are primitive instincts that have remained unchanged. It is probably true that the basic appeal of the rolling downlands is a biological, sexual association of ideas.

Jellicoe's commission was to remodel the landscape and he decided to pick up on

1 *Henry Moore*, Herbert Read, The World of Art Library, Thames and Hudson, 1965, pp146-7.

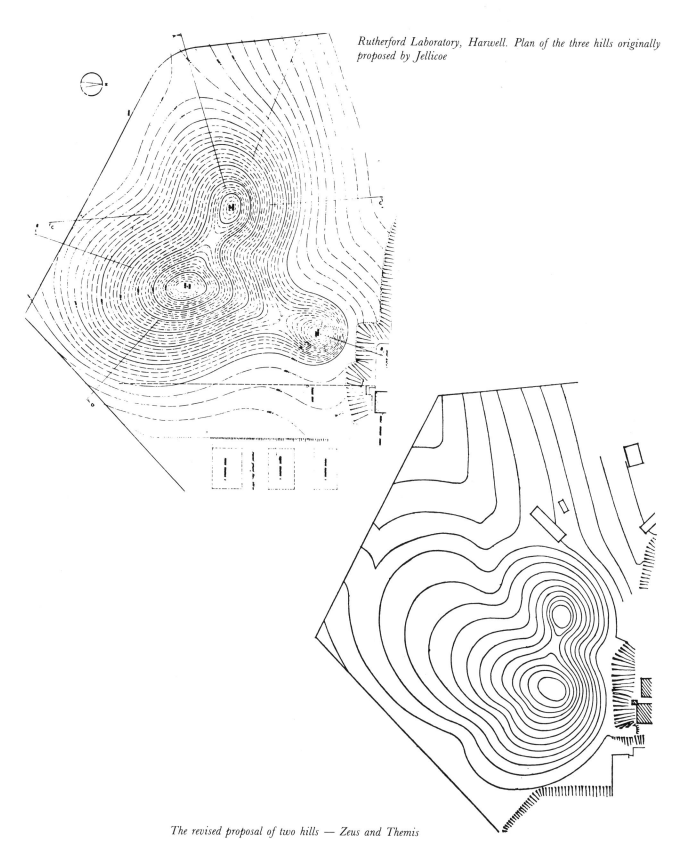

Rutherford Laboratory, Harwell. Plan of the three hills originally proposed by Jellicoe

The revised proposal of two hills — Zeus and Themis

The completed landworks at Harwell

the gently undulating spur of the downs, where the massive chalk tip caused by excavation for Nimrod (the atomic particle accelerator) had been dumped, and create a related land form. He first attempted one hill, and then made a model showing three. At working drawing stage each was given a name for identity. The largest hill became Zeus; the second was named Themis, after one of Zeus' wives, while the third was named Klotho, one of the Fates and the daughter of Zeus and Themis. Klotho was also the Fate able to determine the life and death of man. The symbolism, while reminiscent of family grouping, seemed to be more than relevant on a nuclear energy site. Then, ironically, the experts decreed that Klotho had to go; she would be interfering with the rays emanating from Nimrod. As Jellicoe recalls: 'Klotho then vanished from the scene: Zeus and Themis have correspondingly increased in stature; and the fate of man is still in the balance'.

Jellicoe insisted on allowing the tractor drivers to shape the hills with reasonable freedom, explaining that the spirit of the design was what mattered, not exact compliance with the drawings supplied. The model was the natural concave and convex curves of the adjoining hills. The men understood. The result exceeded

Ben Nicholson's 'Painted Relief', 1943-4, an influence on Jellicoe in his landscaping for the Oldbury-on-Severn nuclear power station site

Aerial view of the Oldbury site before development, 1960

The pilot design for the Oldbury site; this was partially executed

even the most optimistic expectations of the landscape architect.

Oldbury was a flat and estuarial site for a nuclear power station. Three quarters of a million tons of soil from the bed of the Severn, excavated to form a reservoir of cooling water, needed to be disposed of adjacently around the power station. The design was commissioned by the Central Electricity Generating Board as a pilot guide to consortia competing for construction of the entire project.

Jellicoe's intended solution was to create, by means of an arrangement of abstract flat shapes, a link in scale between the mass of the nuclear power station and the random but explicit pattern of surrounding agriculture. Ben Nicholson's abstract geometry of form, and its subtle adjustments, demonstrated that on a large format the smallest realignment of shape can be crucial, and Jellicoe sought to apply the same degree of skill on a landscape format.

In both the Harwell and Oldbury landscapes, Jellicoe realised that he had been designing landscape as an art form on a major scale, guided always by the human condition and more and more aware of its corresponding reliance upon the subconscious. With these schemes he was working again at the forefront of contemporary culture, aware of the needs and requirements of society in the 1960s.

John F Kennedy was assassinated on 22 November 1963. It was a tremor that

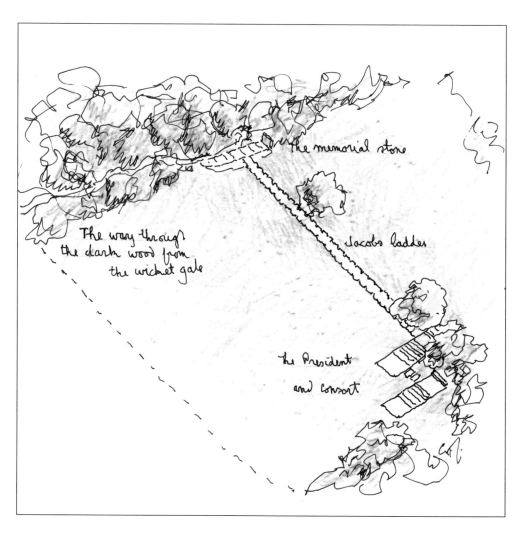

The way through the dark wood from the wicket gate

The memorial stone

Jacobs ladder

The President and Consort

Drawing by Geoffrey Jellicoe of the Kennedy Memorial site, Runnymede. The sketch describes the hidden allegory: the way to the memorial stone starts in a dark wood, and climbs up, emerging into an open area with a view over the Thames

Entrance to the pilgrims' path, Runnymede

The path to the Kennedy Memorial climbs steeply, and the memorial is seen only obliquely at first

View across the lush river meadows to the Thames, Runnymede

shook the world. Almost immediately the British Government designated a small parcel of land, an acre of England, on the slopes above the meadows of Runnymede, beside the Thames. This acre was to be a gift to the United States in memory of the man who had dedicated his life to the pursuit of peace across the world. It was a great and powerful concept. The funds were limited since the bulk of the memorial money was to be for intercountry scholarships.

Jellicoe's problem was to create a sense of grandeur greater than the conditions of budget and site allowed, and with this in mind he decided to rely on analogy. He felt that the story of John Bunyan's *Pilgrim's Progress* would raise the purpose and meaning of the site above the familiar riverside location to realise a universal idea incorporating life, death and the spirit of man. The problem was that the site was small. Rather than regress into a bounded memorial garden with flowers, Jellicoe chose to lay all the emphasis on the route: passing through a wicket gate, leading through a dark wood, it would climb a long winding path.

This path is composed of some 60,000 setts of axe-hewn granite, laid with deliberate irregularity, and laid dry. At any one time there are a few less, since pilgrims' souvenirs tend to accompany pilgrims: an understandable yearning for the memento. The memorial functions at all seasons of the year. In winter the path through the wood is dark as the wood of Dante; in spring the blossoms fall on the setts like flurries of Boston snow; summer comes with myriad greens through the regenerating woodland; in autumn one walks up a carpet of dead leaves. The path is steep and the memorial stone is first glimpsed obliquely. Behind it Jellicoe planted an American scarlet oak which is in colour in November, the month of Kennedy's death.

There is no supervision and security is never required. Parallel to the stone and the river is a detached terrace walk leading along to outsize stone seats, set apart.

At Runnymede, Jellicoe achieved a reductivist yet heroic visual presence, one that transcends. It is a project that, however small, is not a garden but a landscape.

In the later stages of Jellicoe's career there came a divide which marked the end of the landscapist's official work, or so it seemed. Honoured with a knighthood in 1979, Jellicoe himself admits that the attractions of the garden at Grove Terrace, now itself in the ultimate stage of development, seemed paramount both to himself and to Susan Jellicoe. This was not to be.

In the much-loved sanctuary of Grove Terrace, which the Jellicoes had brought to full fruition over nearly forty-five years of care and good husbandry, the chairs below the full-grown trees seemed to beckon in high summer. Over the same period, Jellicoe saw a trenchant comparison between the designs he had made for Ditchley Park in 1936, and the proposals for Hartwell House which he made in 1979. To Jellicoe they represented the remarkable change in attitudes towards the whole environment which he had observed occurring over this period. 1979 was indeed a turning point.

Grove Terrace might be interpreted as a microcosm, but Hartwell was on a universal scale of importance. And Ditchley and Hartwell are so close to each other (both were once owned by the same family) that they invite comparison. The architect James Gibbs was commissioned to build the first for the Lee family, and

The memorial stone at Runnymede

Seat designed by Geoffrey Jellicoe, Kennedy Memorial, Runnymede

Balthasar Nebot, view across the east elevation towards the Gibbs pavilion, Hartwell House, c 1738

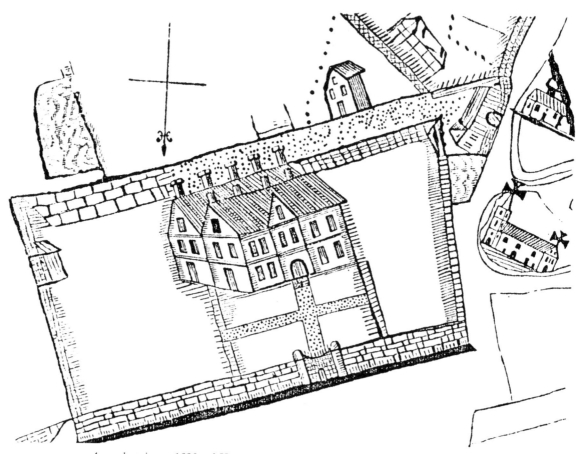

An early print, c 1630, of Hartwell House

*Balthasar Nebot, view from
the column commemorating
George II, Hartwell House,
c 1738*

*Balthasar Nebot, view of
the gardens at Hartwell
House with a conjectural
project for a topiary scheme*

Hartwell House, the south elevation in 1827

soon became bound up in the schemes for the second.

In 1979, therefore, Jellicoe foresook his leafy Highgate garden for a new and critical challenge. And just as James Gibbs moved from Ditchley Park to become inextricably bound up with Hartwell House, so was Jellicoe inexorably drawn to this fresh challenge. For in the way that Ditchley had, as we have seen, launched Jellicoe on a rapid surge of progress in the 1930s (ironically in his sympathetic response to its very classicism), so did Hartwell force through a major realignment in his thinking that had a profound influence well beyond the 1970s.

James Gibbs had been called to Hartwell in the years immediately following 1730 to remodel an earlier building in a Palladian style. However, as early seventeenth century prints show (page 108), the directness of the Jacobean mansion in its formalised forecourt seemed already to be vying with the complexity inherent in its surroundings. It was those surrounding landscape elements which particularly interested Gibbs. Something of an elaborate intellectual game appears to have developed, heightened by the commissioning of twelve imaginative paintings of the house and its surroundings: Balthasar Nebot's fantastic complementary renderings to Gibbs' imaginations for a classical garden around Hartwell House offered a high-water mark for classical garden design in England. The grand design of Gibbs, as thus embellished by Nebot, draws in all possible interest from the surrounding environment overlooking the Vale of Aylesbury to emphasise the distant spire of Aylesbury church.

As for the Jacobean mansion itself, subsequent south and east facades were soon to mask this great Jacobean pile. Hartwell House was enlarged when the owner's heiress had given her husband Sir Thomas Lee, Bart, not only twenty-four children but also some of the most fertile land in the Vale of Aylesbury.

In fact, Hartwell House was created as something of a celebration of fertility generally, a mood to which Gibbs responded with alacrity. A superb classical pavilion which still exists today, became the focus of one view, to be followed by a fine bridge, about 1780, on a distant focal point. Nebot, not to be outdone, painted a canal between the two which has caused more than one speculative but fruitless excavation.

It is now not so much the house that creates interest as the various visual events

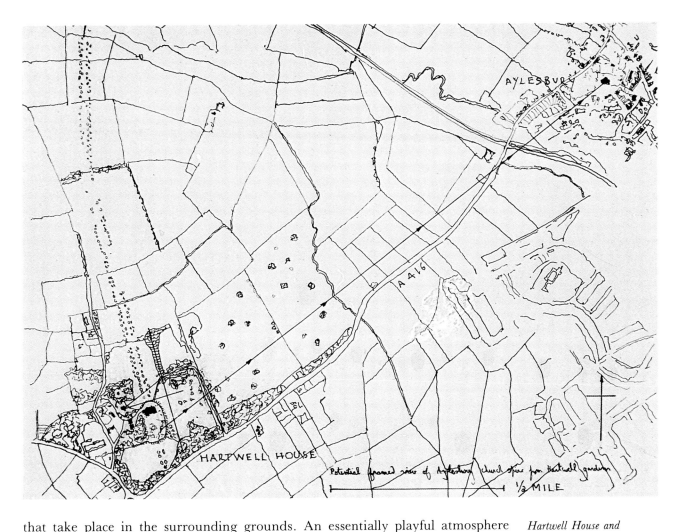

Within the map: AYLESBURY · A 4/6 · HARTWELL HOUSE · Potential framed view of Aylesbury church spire from Hartwell garden · ½ MILE

Hartwell House and environs; drawing by Geoffrey Jellicoe showing the relationship of the house to the spire of Aylesbury church

that take place in the surrounding grounds. An essentially playful atmosphere concurs with the celebratory disposition of the house. If any work of art is to be quoted here for comparison it is probably a film. In 1983 the film 'The Draughtsman's Contract' by Peter Greenaway regaled bemused audiences with an early eighteenth century drama set in an interesting Jacobean house surrounded by a classical-romantic landscape of garden, moat and parklands. The draughtsman of the contract was commissioned to prepare twelve views which comprised the underlying structure of the film; this structure would help the viewer comprehend the environment, the star and subject of the film. As a contemporary director and artist, Greenaway draws the viewer into this structured world as centred on the house and opened up by its twelve specific views, while at the same time releasing the viewer and thereby enabling him to begin to unravel the mystery, to search for meaning.

It appears that Jellicoe, following Gibbs' games, realised that over time the picture presented by Hartwell House had become too confusing with its several layers of meaning, and sought to resolve matters by recourse to a similar clarity of structure.

The conceptual first survey he executed reveals the key elements as they now are: the eighteenth century gothic revival parish church (page 112); the castellated tower; the site of the eighteenth century bridge; the column commemorating George II; the Gibbs pavilion (page 112); the equestrian statue of Frederick, Prince of Wales; and the sculpture placed by Gibbs. All of these elements draw

The parish church designed by Keene is a gothic revival style, 1753. Both this and the next illustration of the grounds at Hartwell House show elements from the past both identified in Jellicoe's 1989 survey

The pavilion designed by Gibbs

one's eye and mind away from the house — which, since Henry Keene's mid-eighteenth century classical addition was built, seems just as well. But now the focus was to be once again upon the centre. As Jellicoe says, 'the half century between 1777 and 1827 admirably reflects the confusion of landscape ideas prevalent in the country as a whole'. This focus became a question of reversal and of a strong articulation inwards to the centre — Hartwell House itself.

In his plan, therefore, Jellicoe sought to reveal the essential evidence of landscape history inherent in the grounds (that is the classical geometry practised from the Jacobean period which still dominates, interwoven with those elements of the heroic-romantic that remain), while still allowing the later 'gardenesque' paths to survive. At a practical level he reorganised the car parking to avoid excess. Most importantly, he restored to view from the stable entrance the equestrian statue of Frederick (as evident in a plan of 1777); he dignified the Gibbs pavilion (his term) by clipped hedges, so framing a potentially fine picture of the bridge and lake beyond; in respect for Nebot he opened up the outward view of Aylesbury church spire and restored the clearly essential views *inwards* to the house as lying well and securely within the underlying and original triangulated structure. Jellicoe here fulfils the role of the draughtsman with the contract: by a known structure he removes the conflicts but cannot but reveal the truth in time and space. The mystery reverts to the house itself.

In another example, Jellicoe refers to the temporal and the spiritual, as he says, conversing: Jacobean house and neo-gothic church may exchange views across the expanse, but Victorian muddle of circular pool must go. Otherwise, he seeks to preserve the continuum of history, allowing future amendment where appropriate to the overall tapestry of landscape history now clarified and preserved.

In November 1989, Jellicoe was invited back to Hartwell (now superbly restored as a hotel) by the new inhabitants and their landlords, the Cook Trust, who prompted him to prepare a further development on the approach to the Gibbs pavilion, and this he proposed to be balanced by a cascade launching downwards from the elevated ground to the south (page 108). Hartwell, Jellicoe himself will admit, was an exercise of some complexity. Clearly it was an eminently post-modern concept and, as such, marks the emergence of the designer as one who has made the transition in philosophy across the years from 1936, to confront without nostalgia the new perspectives of the 1980s and beyond. There is no grand design, as at Ditchley. Here Jellicoe's preoccupations are multivalent, and the solutions proposed more accommodating to history's own varied perspectives. There can be no one solution, only a series of related possibilities towards a solution. With this remarkable project, Jellicoe could move forward a decade, ahead of his rivals, searching for the roots of landscape philosophy. Regrettably the project was not accepted.

Hartwell House is a transitional piece, yet it bears all the signs of a master at work. The designer is in a relaxed and all-embracing mood, gently coaxing his elements into play here and there, yet ruthlessly eliminating the non-essential. Such a landscape is a distillation of history. Gibbs, Nebot and Jellicoe discourse in harmony at Hartwell.

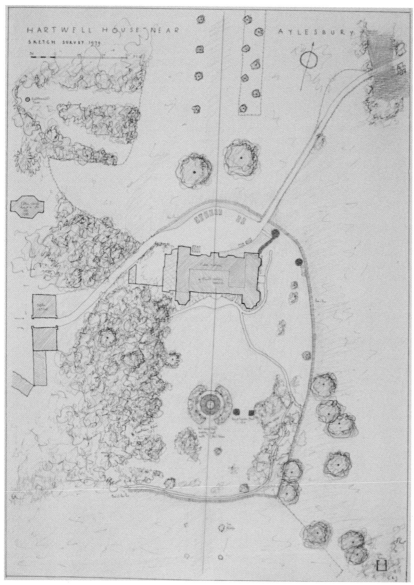

Opposite: Sir Geoffrey Jellicoe's 1989 scheme for the gardens at Hartwell House expands the theme which he first established in 1979, relating the area to the south and east of the house together within the whole complex as it had developed over history

To the south, the visual anomaly posed by the Victorian circular pool had been removed, but an unresolved void had resulted which did nothing for the approach to the Gibbs Pavilion (bottom right of the plan).

Jellicoe has recharged the edges bordering the open lawn opposite the south elevation in a wholly unanticipated manner. First, to the immediate west, on the existing gradient, he has inserted a superb cascade. Second, to the east opposite, he has carefully restructured and enlarged the existing wild 'bosco' on the approach to the Gibbs pavilion, with the addition of a new garden. While the Gibbs Pavilion celebrated 'Wisdom' in the classical sense, Jellicoe has not been side-tracked into any elaboration of the vista into the canal there proposed by Nebot, which would have emphasised man's control over nature. In the 1990s, this carries little scope for fantasy. Instead, from the 'bosco' (no less tamed on plan), there leaps the form of a mythic fish (salmon or dolphin), the creature celebrated by both Roman and Celt as the repository of divine wisdom. The hotel guest can now pass along and through this landscaped form on returning to the hotel terrace.

Meanwhile the terrace itself is upgraded by the installation of eight scented lemon trees. At the head of the fish garden, the creature's watery 'eye' is perfectly balanced by the lateral focus of the circular fountain pool at the climax of the cascade opposite. Under the spread of the lemon trees, the guests' tables and chairs are drawn up. The fantasy, primordial but also postprandial, is complete

Hartwell House and its immediate surroundings prior to Jellicoe's first proposals

Photograph of Hartwell House; the gothic church is back left

114

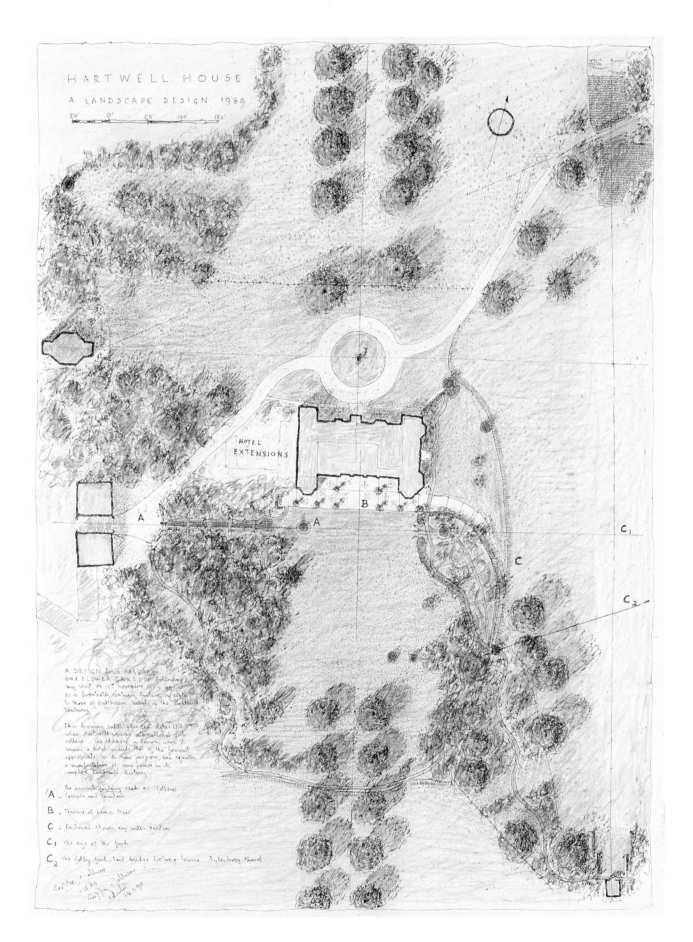

HARTWELL HOUSE

A LANDSCAPE DESIGN 1989

HOTEL
EXTENSIONS

A

A

B

C₁

C

C₂

A DESIGN for a CASCADE
and FLOWER GARDEN following
'my visit on 10ᵗʰ November' to give
as a twentieth century contency in scale
to those of Harthapes habit in the Eighteenth
century

This drawing supersedes the date 1988
when that with various international sub
edition. The changes in design when it
became a hotel include that of the present
appropriate for its new purpose, are equally
a manifestation of some peness in it
complex landscape history.

the present features reads as follows

'A - Cascade and fountain

B - Terrace of Linden trees

C - Enclosed Flower and water garden

C₁ - The edge of the park

C₂ - The folly foot-seat bridge looking towards Aylesbury church

CHAPTER 6
SHUTE: A GARDEN LABORATORY

'It is the recurrent interaction of the several parts with the whole that stretches one's perception and hence one's imagination. This is not simply the conjunction of intelligent planting with views beyond. This garden can replenish the mind itself, no less. That is its purpose'

The garden design for Shute House, Donhead St Mary, near Shaftesbury in Wiltshire, was commissioned from Geoffrey Jellicoe in 1972. The house itself stands high upon an open escarpment, while the village road runs by hard upon the main entrance. Away to the north are long perspectives. But most striking of all are the direct views of the downs, both from the house and as laid out within the overall scheme of things, southwards and to the south-east line of the horizon.

Shute's special qualities derive from a range of peculiarities of geology and topography. The garden is seven hundred feet above sea level, and sited on greensand — a glauconitic sandstone that weathers to engender a good, light, well-drained if acidic soil. It occupies an ancient site in that part of England which most readily reveals the prehistoric, and the area has been settled over a very lengthy period. Fully aware of an ancient, even primeval history here, and coming upon the place from the higher planes of Palladianism, the present owners drew as their starting point not the house itself but the mysterious spring, which rises as the source of the river Nader, on the western side of the site. Michael Tree (Ronald and Nancy Tree's son) and his wife Lady Anne Tree had moved from Mereworth Castle, Kent, a masterpiece of the architect Colen Campbell, which Michael Tree had inherited. While there had been little that could be changed at Mereworth, so tight were the strictures of Palladianism, they found that circumstances at Shute were wholly different. And although they brought with them from Mereworth a great appreciation of classical design, at Shute they wished to search even further back to the very essence of landscape design.

There was no question in their minds that Geoffrey Jellicoe would be the right person to commission, since in any case he had worked so successfully for Michael's father. There was little Jellicoe had felt able to do at Mereworth, viewing it when asked very much as a *fait accompli.* In any case he was then over seventy, an age when most of his contemporaries had retired.

But as soon as Jellicoe had made a first visit, he realised that Shute presented a remarkable opportunity, and that if his ideas were to work it would only be in the fullest collaboration with the Trees. He took the view that Shute was a great experiment, and that from the beginning all three of them had to take a long view and allow the project to mature over several years. Shute, in fact, has become the laboratory of Jellicoe's ideas, and development is still in progress.

The primary element in Jellicoe's apparatus has, of course, been water in all its various forms and ways. Since this has characterised his fundamental methodology from his earliest projects in the 1930s, such a resource as he found at Shute was a massive bonus. Emanating from the spring itself, and making maximum use of the existing gradient and its related pools, the flow is guided by Jellicoe through a unique sequence of watercourses, spilling in one form and another southwards towards a wholly unexpected climax in the pasture beyond, yet at the same time fully augmenting an existing but rather purposeless reservoir at the top of the site, which becomes a separate, formal canal of a wholly classical dimension. This, although an important and powerful gesture, remains secondary, a diversion — even *divertimento* — from the downward thrust of the spring water's natural flow through no less than seven varied pools.

The formal genesis is, however, the visitor's first surprise: to his immediate left as he enters the garden, a long gravity-fed sequence of bubble fountains push down through lush plantations; this rill directs the eye down its course. It provides the rushing sound of water as an artificial premonition, by way of introduction, of the ultimate direction of the naturally-flowing courses and pools elsewhere in the garden that meander in another way towards the open landscape.

The second structuring device which Jellicoe uses at Shute is that of the overlapping vista. The first view of the downs is repeated as the path doubles back on a higher plane. This is complemented by a series of counter-axes, points of interest and secondary foci (such as statues) that build up towards the formal climax, the set-piece at the head of the canal. In the variety of arbours and private spaces that characterise the primary route, interspersed with occasional figures, it is the recurrent interaction of the several parts with the whole that stretches one's perception and hence one's imagination. This is not simply the conjunction of intelligent planting with views beyond. This garden can replenish the mind itself, no less. That is its purpose.

Nor is this process wholly visual: apart from the continuing variations in light and scent — as with any well-planned garden of the seasons — there is a consciously orchestrated audio-visual complement. Jellicoe argues that it is theoretically possible to create a true harmonic water chord from four cascades along the rill, and at Shute there was some experimentation using the simplest of devices, copper V-forms set in concrete. Theoretically, as the number of Vs is increased, the alto tone lightens and rises up the scale as the water falls with increasing fragmentation more and more lightly on the calm water below.

Rising therefore from its source at the spring (the highest pool) the water runs southwards by two routes, the classical way combining canal and rill, and the romantic route via a lower pool and temple. The cascades here are formed from selected horizontal stones, the laying and setting of which was carefully detailed by Geoffrey Jellicoe.

The two courses are reunited on entering the bog garden. But the sound of falling and running water (as distinct from the stillness at the canal) is not the only sound. High on this ridge, Shute catches every passing breeze, and even on the stillest of summer days there is the varied rustling of leaves and branches, an effect

View of Shute House, Wiltshire, from the south

The landscape of Shute looking north: the house and grounds are approximately centre left of the photograph

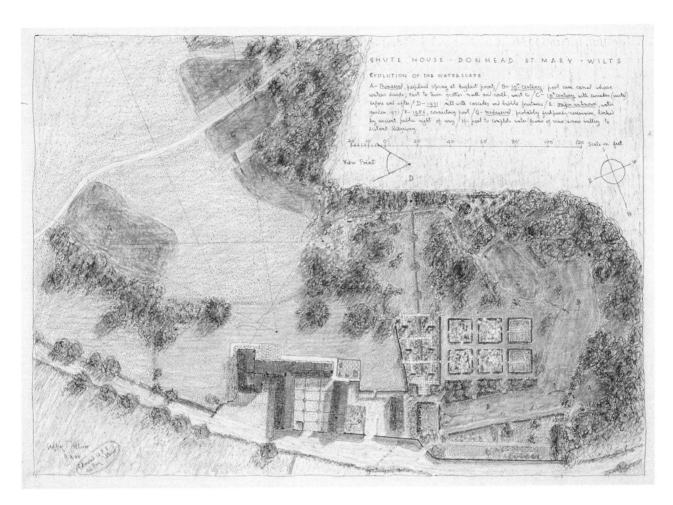

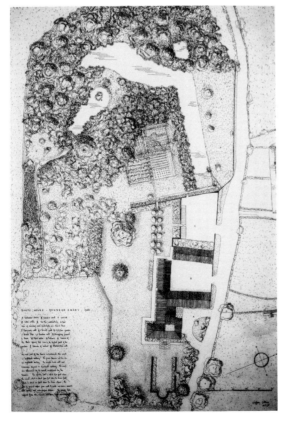

Shute: drawing by Geoffrey Jellicoe of the grounds in 1988

Shute: drawing by Geoffrey Jellicoe of the house and grounds before alteration, 1968

The source of the river Nader, Shute: the spring with underwater moss landscape

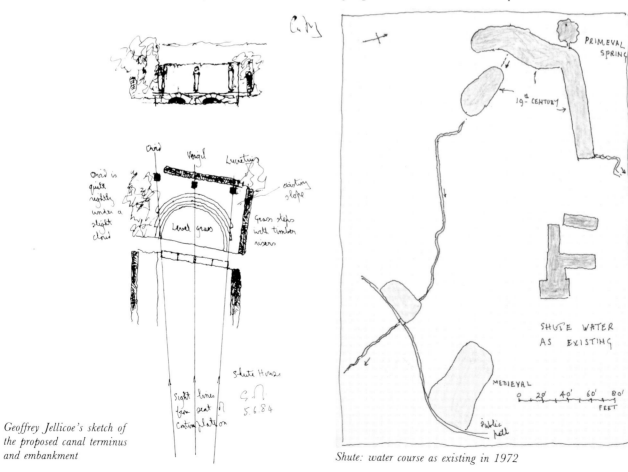

Geoffrey Jellicoe's sketch of the proposed canal terminus and embankment

Shute: water course as existing in 1972

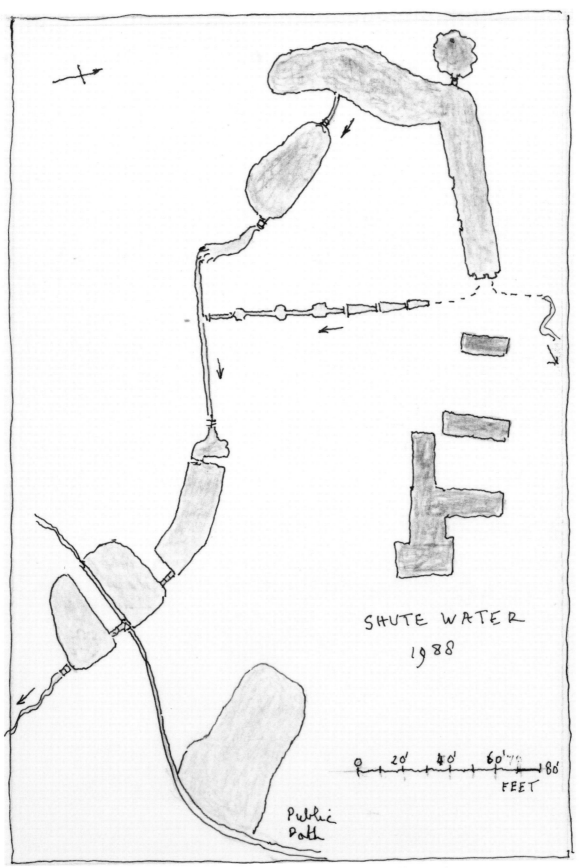

SHUTE WATER
1988

Public
Path

The water course at Shute as proposed and drawn by Geoffrey Jellicoe. The main additions can be seen on
the lower left, with the rill above to the right

First orientation in the Shute landscape: looking down the rill

Views of the canal, that on the right from the source of the spring

Two views of the canal: top, points of interest, such as statues, are used by Jellicoe along the canal to build up interest before the final climax — the formal set-piece at the head of the canal, above

123

Jellicoe and Michael and Anne Tree are particularly aware of.

Such sounds of wind and water are cherished by film directors such as Antonioni or Bergman. Invariably, however, they are reduced to singling out a single elemental sound (water, wind) and enlarging it to the exclusion of all else. At Shute, Anne Tree's exposition on this subject reminds one of the efforts of the Russian film director Andrey Tarkovsky to capture these myriad sounds in his film 'Mirror':

> We wanted the sound to be close to that of an earthly echo, filled with poetic suggestion — to rustling, to sighing. The notes had to convey the fact that reality is conditional, and at the same time accurately to reproduce precise states of mind, the sounds of a person's interior world.[1]

To provide this earthly echo, Tarkovsky was obliged to rely on electronic music. For it is only in the reality of such a garden as Shute that such natural expressions of nature in all seasons can be attuned to the mind.

It is in the passage of the seasons that a garden or landscape design must pass its fullest test. Shute has been realised by Geoffrey Jellicoe together with Anne and Michael Tree on just such an ambitious basis, and their mutual perception has been well rewarded: the 'earthly echo' joins with the symphonic variations of the water in developing visual sequences for the mind's eye to catch and ponder.

Shute's garden fulfils all these aspirations in barely three acres. In this respect it is very much a garden of our age. Here a series of gardens interact: a water garden, a bog garden, large plantings of camellias, surrounding woodland, and a box garden of six squared divisions, each to contain specific and traditionally English herbaceous plants, where blue meets mauve, mauve pink, and pink red, at the centre of each square an apple tree to bear fruit from its blossom (the trees are not intended to be primarily or solely ornamental). An orchard on the south of the box garden is underplanted with narcissi and Lenten lilies. Beyond this, a large Italianate statue stands serenely under a fine rowan tree; below runs the deep pool of the romantic route fringed with the rose 'Frau Dagmar Hastrup'. Close to the spring itself *Rhododendron ponticum* seems no longer out of place, as in so many gardens. Arum lilies flourish behind.

In the spring of 1988, Michael and Anne Tree again invited Geoffrey Jellicoe to Shute to help, with fine timing, in the resolution of the southern extremes of the garden. 'The Garden Allegory...The Metamorphosis of Classicism into Romanticism' closes the edge of the waterscape, the 'ultima thule' of Shute. Jellicoe's seemingly ambitious title indicates the importance of this addition. Passing southwards after the canal, there is a brief foretaste of this *manierismo* in the triangular grove of ilex where perspective narrows dramatically. This was inserted by Jellicoe as a 'hinge' in the articulation of a garden plan designed to catch the unwary as one stoops below the branches to see the path down and beyond through the pure geometry of the box parterre. Like the rustle in leaves that foretells rain, the mind is brushed with a question mark, and one quickens one's pace. Can the serenity of immutable classicism be sustained?

At the end of the sequence, Jellicoe has provided the answer. Reaching the 'Garden Allegory', which if one follows the path is unavoidable, and where one

1 *Sculpting in Time: Reflections on the Cinema*, Andrey Tarkovsky, translated from the Russian by Kitty Hunter-Blair, Bodley Head, 1986, p162.

A garden allegory. This project was completed in outline in 1988 and Jellicoe here expresses his yearning for the allegorical landscape by means of the transformation of an existing classical composition into a highly charged play on romanticism. In this vignette, still in progress, the players emerge in the form of giant figures in yew (D), an exaggeratedly tall ivy steeple (E) and the mysterious chest (C). The climax, however, is found in the western apex of the site in the form of a large block of reflective crystalline rock (F). The ivy-consumed temple is at A, and the laurel tunnel entrance to the site at B, both already there in 1988

might expect to find either compost heaps or a jungle, tucked into the adjacent dead space a new formalism confronts the visitor, a parable of the post-modern.

This 'Garden Allegory' works best in the early evening when silence deepens, ideally in late September, when leaves are turning and there is a change in the air, or when the summer sun still moves round increasing the shadows of the trees. In winter its powers can be felt in mid-afternoon on a clear day as mist creeps in.

Entering through a laurel tunnel, another triangular space is now revealed, overlooked by an ivy-consumed temple which remains significantly peripheral. Here, interpreting a sketch from Anne Tree, Jellicoe has inserted a 'chest' made of English boxwood and a mysterious steeple of ivy. Between this and the temple are seven menacing allegorical figures, slightly larger than human scale. At the western extreme of the area is a massive block of reflective, crystalline rock, and there the westering sun catches the faceted surface of the rock, arousing a suspicion

The bog garden, Shute, where the classical and romantic water courses are reunited

The alto cascade at Shute

The mysterious triangular plantation between the canal and the box parterre at Shute. The space acts as a directional 'hinge' to align the grid of the box garden

The laurel tunnel at Shute: following the romantic route through the garden, the visitor passes through the tunnel to the 'Garden Allegory'

of alchemy. There is no exit possible. The visitor ultimately must retrace steps, leaving the enclave via the laurel tunnel from whence he or she came, or else escape over the stream on somewhat perilous stepping stones.

Shute pre-dates Jellicoe's work at Sutton Place, the subject of the next chapter. But it also post-dates it, for the project at Sutton Place was never fully realised. At Shute, Jellicoe and the Trees have continued to explore the hold of the subconscious on man's mind in the making of gardens. The ideas have spread through newer projects, further afield. But the laboratory garden of Shute has played a vital, irreplaceable role in the development of Jellicoe's ideas.

CHAPTER 7
SUTTON PLACE AND AFTER

'Sutton Place was the scene of one of the most remarkable experiments in twentieth century patronage. Jellicoe had been presented with a unique opportunity to work out in the post-modern era certain ideas about landscape as art'

In 1980, shortly after completing the proposals for Hartwell House, and parallel to developments at Shute, Geoffrey Jellicoe was commissioned by the American Stanley Seeger to design the gardens at Sutton Place, near Guildford, a Tudor house previously owned by the eccentric oil magnate Paul Getty. (In 1986 the property was sold to another American, Edward Koch.) Between 1980 and 1986 considerable progress was made to carry out Jellicoe's plans, and what has been completed stands today mostly as he intended.

The design approach that Jellicoe pursued at Sutton Place was essentially pragmatic, yet it incorporates something of the historicist discipline of his earlier garden designs. The experience of Hartwell had led him into new gardens of the mind, and clearly the process of composition within the existing content of Sutton Place was a major challenge.

One aspect was very different at Sutton Place however: the cultural grasp and contemporary sympathies of the client. Stanley Seeger is an example of the rare individual patron who, while holding the excellence of historical architecture and landscape at a high premium, demonstrates his achievement and confidence in his own time by interrelating the present with the past. Such endeavour demands skills of the highest order in carrying out such an integration.[1]

Jellicoe claims that, in financial value of work, Sutton Place was worth more than all his previous garden projects together. But that does not seem to have been the main attraction, for Jellicoe has also been adept at turning jobs down if they seem unsuitable. At Sutton Place, however, there seemed to be an unusual degree of intellectual parity. Seeger certainly understood immediately what Jellicoe meant when he spoke of expressing the subconscious element in art. They understood each other about twentieth century art too — Jellicoe had by now been a Trustee of the Tate Gallery for some years. Seeger shared Jellicoe's admiration for two direct contemporaries, Henry Moore and Ben Nicholson, while Jellicoe understood Seeger's feeling for the paintings of Claude Monet and René Magritte. Both designer and client agreed on the need for excellence in every aspect of technique and materials. Not only was there a potential for designed landscape, but equally for building a genuine ecology.

Accordingly, Geoffrey Jellicoe wasted no time in getting down to the drawing board. He was fortunate to be able to rely upon Susan Jellicoe for the planting

1. The architect Sir Hugh Casson, who had already been engaged on the internal works at Sutton Place, had introduced Jellicoe to Stanley Seeger.

plan; and he engaged Marian Thompson, on very precise terms, to draw up an ecological plan for the whole estate. The terms of reference she was given were:

> To study the present ecology of the area between the walled gardens and the fringe farmland, and present scientific proposals as a basis of landscape art.

This depth of enquiry is typical of the degree to which Geoffrey Jellicoe will go to identify the special characteristics of a site, in both scientific and artistic terms. He also chose to draw the boundaries of this brief as widely as possible to include all the land around Sutton Place over which Stanley Seeger had control and under management policies. In this way Jellicoe ensured that the scale of operations which he was to pursue would occur within a balanced system in nature, one that would continue to thrive on a natural range of flora and fauna.

Jellicoe's first visit to Sutton Place was on 22 July 1980. A considerable transformation had already occurred within the house, and Seeger had managed to disperse some of the customary Getty gloom. Part of Seeger's collection of twentieth century works was already evident, indicating an optimism about the future as well as a respect for the past. In a very short space of time Jellicoe had the basis of an idea; after four days of consideration and one spent at the drawing board, a diagrammatic scheme was approved by Stanley Seeger virtually on sight. The plan was uncomplicated: existing axes were retained (as at Hartwell) and the house itself was readily reconciled with the vastly implemented landscape about it. Jellicoe claims that:

> The scheme is primarily a reaffirmation of classical values, enriched and not disrupted by romanticism (as the intangibles are still classified). There was no thought at this stage as to what those intangibles might be.

Jellicoe credits the client, at this stage, with two major decisions: that the Moore lake landscape, repositioned by him, and the Nicholson wall chosen by him, should be gigantic in scale, well beyond the domestic English character of the house. This was the germ of the idea of a grand allegory, 'of creation, life and aspiration'.

Sutton Place, of course, was no stranger to the grand manner. Despite the evident domesticity of the original Tudor building, complete with gatehouse (Jellicoe marked the line of this demolished brick structure with a bed lined by box hedge, filled with variegated pachysandra), a double avenue of limes had existed. The Weston family, the original builders, were among the first to introduce the Renaissance style to England. No ordinary family, they were distinguished by their cosmopolitanism. Furthermore, as knights of St John of Jerusalem, they were no strangers to the Mediterranean. Sir Richard Weston, the builder, was an accomplished courtier and friend of Henry VIII. But the family fell from grace; Francis Weston, Sir Richard's son, was caught in the divisive antagonisms that accompanied Anne Boleyn's political decline and Sir Richard was executed, though not before infusing Sutton Place with a lasting potion of Renaissance culture.[2]

Geoffrey Jellicoe's scheme for the gardens involved no major change as built, other than the transfer of the lake from south to north. Apart from the lake, he proposed seven major interventions.

2 *The Renaissance at Sutton Place*, exhibition catalogue, Sutton Place Heritage Trust, 1983, pp10-20.

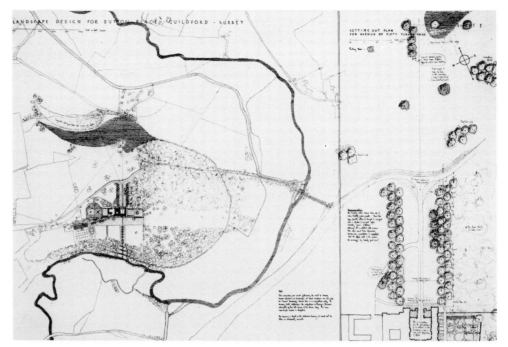

Sutton Place: Geoffrey Jellicoe's proposals, 1980. The drawing is intended to emphasise the relationship of the primeval to modern man. The setting out plan to the right shows fifty oak trees joining the traditionally closed north avenue approach to the house, symbolic of Seeger's fiftieth birthday

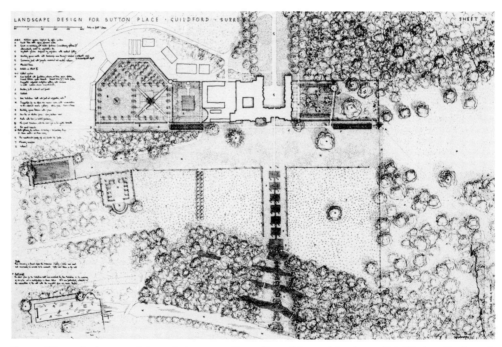

Sutton Place: the house and immediate surroundings. From left to right the walled Kitchen Garden, the swimming pool, the house, the Paradise Garden, the Moss or Secret Garden. The Great Cascade lies at the centre front, while the Nicholson Wall and the open-air music room are centre left

South elevation of the proposals for the grounds of Sutton Place

Sutton Place, the gatehouse range from the courtyard before its demolition in about 1782

First, a walled garden was established to the east, balancing that to the west of the house. From the house, this garden was reached across a newly inserted moat, in fact, a pool for lilies, lined with balustrades bearing a marked similarity to those depicted in Bellini's 'The Earthly Paradise' (see page 73). The walled garden overlooked by these 'three balconies' was appropriately called the Paradise Garden, and beyond it, separated from the Paradise Garden by an existing yew hedge, was the Moss or Secret Garden.

This east walled garden is the epitome of mood. Of Villa Gamberaia's gardens, Jellicoe has said:

There is a place for every mood. Hamlet will find an answering chord in the twilight of the bosco, mysterious, elusive, fantastic with the shapes of the ilex;

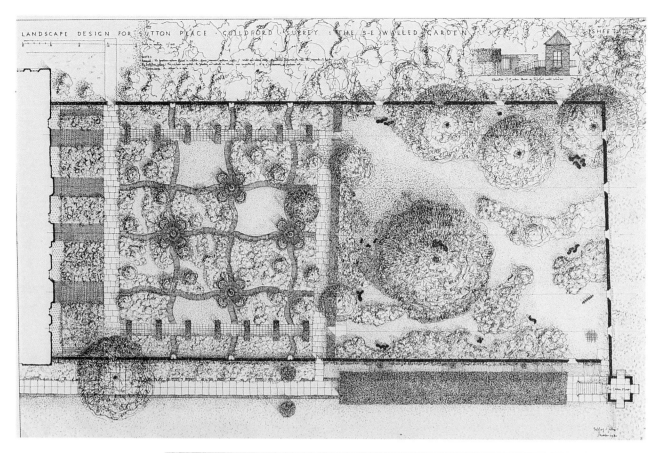

Geoffrey Jellicoe's proposals
for the east walled garden
enclosing the Paradise
Garden and the Moss
Garden. On the left the
balustraded moat leading
from the house

The east end of the house
leading to the Paradise
Garden with balustrades
after Bellini

132

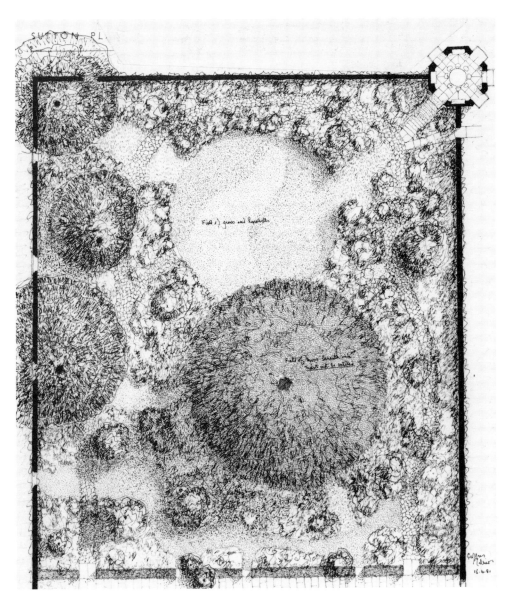

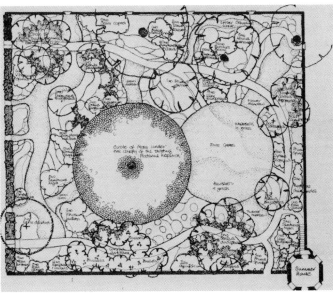

The Moss Garden at Sutton Place with its two intersecting circles of moss and grass, the former under a massive London plane

Planting plan for the Moss Garden carried out by Susan Jellicoe and Hilary Shrive

The Magritte Walk — a surrealistic terminus at the end of the long South Walk

the joker can go and joke among the water steps and grotto; and the two can agree to differ in the most delightful of lemon gardens.

In the Paradise Garden today Hamlet would find today a pleasure garden replete with perfumed blooms, arbours for discourse, and fountains offering both a degree of privacy in conversation and a quality of sensuality. Grass glades are for contemplation: Jellicoe has created a true pleasance where the natural sounds of water, bees and birds mingle together in a beguiling symphony...amidst honeysuckle, jasmin, roses and *Clematis armandii.*

The paths are sinuous, and yet there is a wavy grid of ways leading on down to the Moss Garden. Here Jellicoe draws upon his own memories of childhood to derive an atmosphere of seclusion and mystery. Two intersecting circles structure the available space, one is open and accessible grass, the other lies below a massive London plane tree and is covered with mosses. Groups of wild flowers are encouraged to grow naturally. Bulbs are also planted — bluebells, autumn crocus, and certain rarer items such as *Orchid mascula.* It is rumoured that the moss, leucobryum, is slow to prosper where intended but, paradoxically, has taken to the walls of the Paradise Garden, where it flourishes beneath the spouting masks of Nathan David's 'Ages of Man', forsaking the ecologically sound and deliberate installations of fallen trees.

The second of the major interventions, the long South Walk, acting in fact as a cross-axis (east-west), was planted with pleached limes which now grow into a solid canopy through which the Magritte Walk, a kind of surrealistic terminus, is reached. Here we are treated to a false perspective of Roman urns.

Third, an avenue of fountains, including the Persephone fountain and grottoes, was proposed to form the Great Cascade, with all the existing parkland trees in the immediate area retained (see page 140).

Fourth, an open-air music room or theatre, a green and geometrically significant space, was planned to the west of the Great Cascade. Neither this nor the cascade have yet been established.

Fifth, a walled swimming pool was transformed by Jellicoe, with stepping stones and a kidney-shaped raft, in a playful tribute to the work of the Spanish painter Miro.

Sixth, the existing walled Kitchen Garden, was reorganised by Jellicoe into a place redolent with both the practicalities of husbandry as well as the memories of childhood gardens of this kind.

Finally, the Nicholson Wall, sited at the west end of the garden appears as a heroic and uncompromising symbol, a frozen symphony in Carrara marble, seemingly weightless as reflected in the adjacent pool.

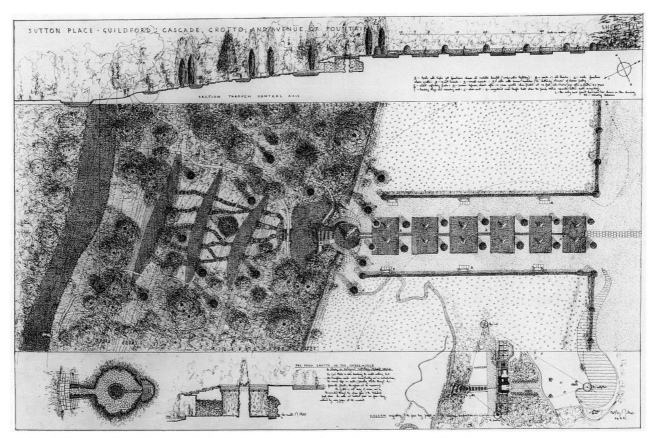

Geoffrey Jellicoe's drawing of his proposals for the Great Cascade at Sutton Place. An avenue of fountains leads to the Persephone fountain, underground grottoes and finally to the river. (See also page 140)

The Nicholson 'White Relief' wall; the great Carrara marble relief is seemingly weightless as reflected in the adjacent pool

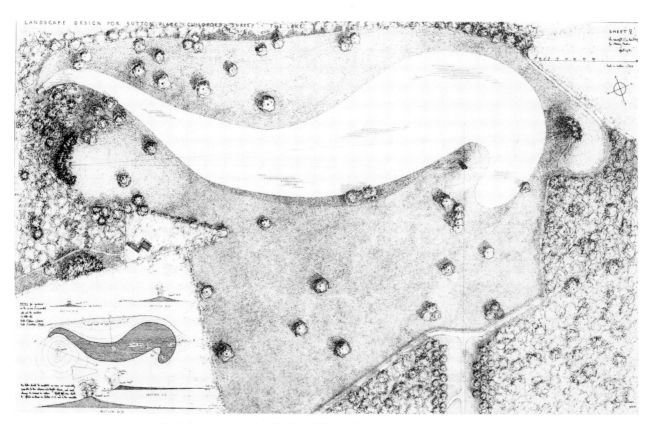

The lake as proposed by Geoffrey Jellicoe. The analogy of its fish-like shape, with hills representing Man, Woman and Child, refers to the Creation

Sutton Place, Guildford: the landscape context

With the Nicholson Wall, Jellicoe reaffirms his early commitment to the white minimalism of the modern movement. Although completed posthumously, this superb work in its setting serves to demonstrate the genius of Nicholson, and Jellicoe saw both this great relief, and the intended work by Henry Moore for the lake site, 'Divided Oval', cast in bronze, as essentially complementary to each other. But this was not to be, and the change of ownership has lost Sutton Place the sculpture that Moore offered for the cost of casting alone.

The lake itself is complete, and making its ecological contribution much as originally intended. Jellicoe has created a fish-like shape with hills representing Man, Woman and Child. The analogy refers to the Creation. It begins the human allegory of Sutton Place.

In these compositions, all of which combine effortlessly to comprise a greater whole, Jellicoe was able to deploy with ease and the full consent of an enlightened client all of his genius for landscape design.

It should be emphasised that the creative span of design, construction and planting at Sutton Place lasted from 1980 until 1986, while in 1982 Stanley Seeger set up the Sutton Place Heritage Trust to administer and protect his creation. Over this period, Sutton Place was the scene of one of the most remarkable experiments in twentieth century patronage that have been documented. Jellicoe had been presented with a unique opportunity to work out in the post-modern era certain ideas about landscape as art which went well beyond the modernist period. And yet, in the grandeur of his approach, and his attitude towards history, Jellicoe

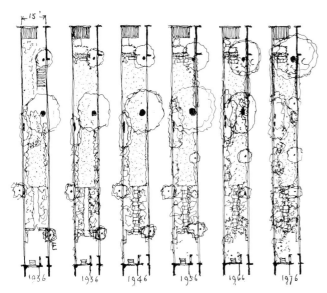

Grove Terrace, Highgate, the garden 1936-76. Geoffrey Jellicoe drew this series of garden plans showing the natural change in tree growth for each decade of development. 'The mood of a garden can appear to have changed of its own accord, imposing its changes of idea imperceptibly upon its owners'

The arbour at the end of the Grove Terrace garden had, by 1976 with growth of trees and shrubs, become a shady giardino segreto *all of fifty paces from the house. Susan and Geoffrey Jellicoe and friend enjoy a respite in high summer*

revealed that a modernist can be a true classicist if he has the perception and the understanding of history.

In all of the allegorical zones or enclaves which Jellicoe placed around the house, concepts are developed which reflect a lifetime of landscape design. He has sustained the original axes of the house, while weaving in a range of visual statements, aspects of the universe. This is a consummation of the philosophy of late twentieth century man. In the distillation, a Renaissance structure is restored and then overlaid with the prevailing influences of the twentieth century as represented by Einstein, Jung and Picasso (see page 141). Landscape, logic and irrationality discourse in harmony. As Jellicoe says:

> All man-made environment is a projection of our psyche, whether individual or collective, and when this is not so (ie a projection of our brain solely) then there is disruption and unhappiness that is mainly due to the dislocation or repression of subconscious instincts.

Jellicoe's thinking here has been close to the view of certain younger architects of the late twentieth century, such as Peter Eisenman. In the post-modern epoch, such designers find the areas where repression is significant; the urge is to structure such characteristics of the psyche into building and to release disruption by expressing it.

At Sutton Place, Jellicoe was able to develop an investigation into such matters which he began at the Kennedy Memorial in order to bring meaning back into landscape and garden design through art.

During this transitional period, Jellicoe welcomed a commission from Sir John Baring, the distinguished merchant banker. His new house, which the architect Francis Pollen had sited close to The Grange, the former house of the Baring family, offered promising scope. Jellicoe took full advantage of the lake that lay below this new site to create an island vantage point (from which the Baring family could be reminded of the Augustan classical presence of The Grange) as well as

View down the garden at Grove Terrace. In this 1954 view, the Jellicoe's love of natural disorder prevails

a typical Jellicoe mound, christened by his client Monte Jellicoe, and similar in purpose to Mount Kronos established in a key location at Cheltenham (see pages 144 and 145).

In the period during which Sutton Place began to materialise, Jellicoe had at last begun to enjoy the full maturity of the garden which he and Susan had developed at Grove Terrace. The lengthening years found them deriving solace and mutual fulfilment in these carefully nurtured surroundings.

Of the garden at Grove Terrace and gardens in general, Jellicoe has written:

A great ash tree split and was finally removed to reveal a self-sown sycamore that had grown tall enough to conceal the silhouette of the houses opposite;

Model of the proposed Great Cascade at Sutton Place. The line of fountains runs from the south of the house to the Persephone fountain, grottoes and river beyond. Parkland trees have been retained

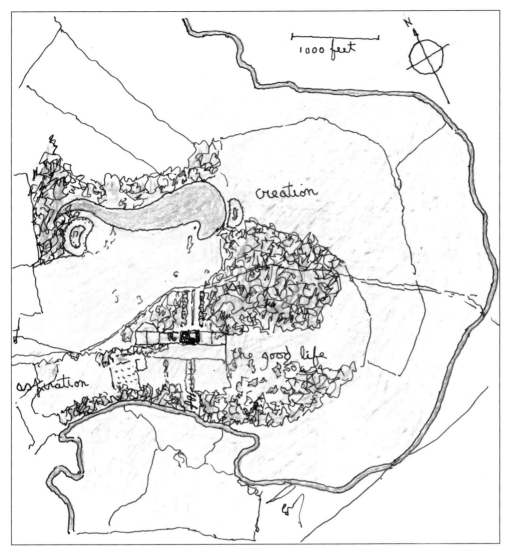

Geoffrey Jellicoe's drawing of Sutton Place illustrating the influence of Jung's work: creation, aspiration and the good life

the fig tree grew vigorously dividing the grass lawn into two parts; similarly, small fruit trees and shrubs closed in to destroy the geometric vista. By 1976 the garden had finally metamorphosed itself from the classical into the romantic. . . It has been argued that a house and garden for every individual family is impossible in a country short of space, but a theoretical calculation shows that a circle with a radius of thirty-five miles from Charing Cross could contain the whole population of Britain at twelve houses to the acre, fully serviced with open spaces including the Thames. The crucial factor is not the space itself, but how the space is disposed.

The community at Grove Terrace was long established. Amongst Jellicoe's friends here were Kenneth Robinson, the former Minster of Health, and Oliver Cox, a former student from the AA days. The gardens were equally distinguished, including Frederick Gibberd's own, as well as one by Christopher Tunnard. The mood was one of congenial but active retirement.

On one occasion, a distinguished visitor arrived by ministerial car with a 'Red Book' by Humphry Repton under his arm. Francis Pym found solace during the

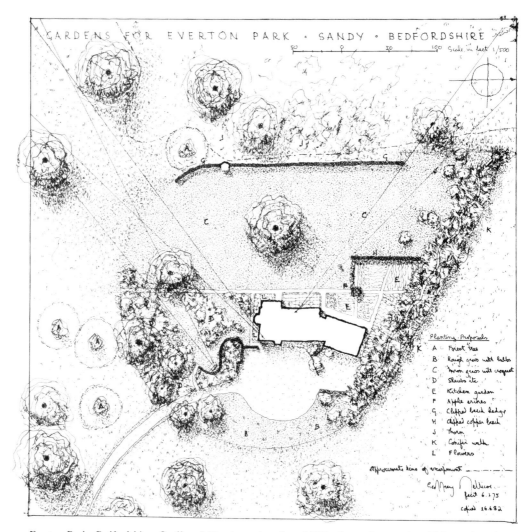

Everton Park, Bedfordshire. Geoffrey Jellicoe's garden plan, 1974, shows the way in which two key views from the house take advantage of the surrounding planting. The view to the left (south) runs from the study window; that to the right (north-west) takes advantage of a gap beyond a clipped beech hedge to reach the open Bedfordshire landscape beyond

travails of the Falklands crisis to escape from the cabinet room (effectively by then a war room) and discuss with Geoffrey and Susan Jellicoe the gardens at Everton Park in Bedfordshire, where in 1974 Jellicoe had laid out an ingenious new space on pasture in the parkland around the Pym's former family home. Now the family had evacuated to a smaller, but possibly better sited place with a fine and long view across the Bedfordshire plain from the high ground above Sandy.

The long involvement of the Pym family with the site, over three centuries, together with the precedent of Repton and this designer's legacy of superb trees, caught Jellicoe's imagination. Francis Pym proved to be a deeply sensitive landowner with a fine sense of detail and a yearning for operational precision, which did not preclude a certain romanticism in his love of gardening. Following leads from Jellicoe, he has developed further areas of the garden with ingenuity. Everton is a place of great trees, without the facility of lake or river. The dry, sandy soil can support well-rooted but deciduous varieties with great success. Three centuries of tree husbandry by a single family have ensured that ancient subconscious affinities prevail. A strikingly long paved way (a familiar Jellicoe

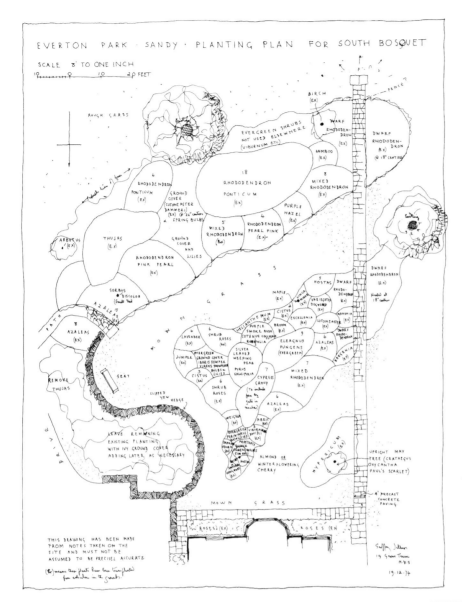

The planting plan drawing is titled:

EVERTON PARK · SANDY · PLANTING PLAN FOR SOUTH BOSQUET

SCALE 8' TO ONE INCH

Everton Park. Detailed planting plan by Susan Jellicoe. The south elevation end of the house, containing the study and drawing room windows, looks on to a lush area of azaleas, mixed rhododendrons, bergenias and shrub roses which have now grown in together to create a solid field of colour in season

A typical Jellicoe element at Everton is the seat, from which the natural disorder inspired by Susan Jellicoe can be contemplated in full privacy from the house

143

Island seat with
distant view of
The Grange

The
cascade
with monte Jellico be

Drawing by Geoffrey
Jellicoe for the project for
Sir John Baring at The
Grange, Hampshire

motif) emphasises the primary north-south axis of the site and skirts the western edge of the new house. Large openings reveal the view to distant horizons in a manner more akin to the high Chilterns at Watlington in Oxfordshire than to this Bedfordshire escarpment. Francis Pym and his wife can enjoy to the full two special and private views from the house — one external, the other from a study window — which soar into the distant park.

Susan Jellicoe's original planting plan has been faithfully pursued, although stragglers have been eliminated.

Revisiting the place in May 1989, Jellicoe was able to celebrate with the Pyms a remarkable fruition of their combined efforts, and to be reminded also of Susan Jellicoe's remarkable skill in complementing his designs with her own planting expertise. The occasion was one of undoubted success. For here certain English stoicisms were seen to be healthily evident. While Jellicoe himself had philosophically suffered the disappointments in one year of both the regression of work at Sutton Place, and the postponement of the Moody Historical Gardens, not to mention the dismantling of the Nevill's important garden as Horsted, Uckfield, at Everton he could realise a sense of genuine achievement, persistent and

section through dining room

The
dining
room

Susan and Geoffrey Jellicoe on the beach in Dorset with his niece Ann Jellicoe (Mayne) and her daughter Katkin, c 1970

Geoffrey Jellicoe gives his great-niece Katkin Mayne an etching lesson, c 1980...

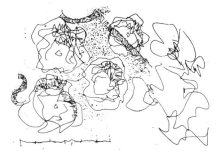

...the result: 'Order Out of Disorder' is the title, though there is no resemblance to any Jellicoe project

progressive over the years. To the Pym family, fifteen years of development against several centuries of survival, suggests generations of propagation to come. And by and large it looked as if this would be followed through along lines which Jellicoe had ordained.

At Everton, too, was solace in the aftermath of Susan's tragic and slow decline from a terminal illness. They moved from Grove Terrace in 1984 forsaking the garden of five decades of happiness. In a typical Jellicoe arrangement, however, they moved forward, into Berthold Lubetkin's modernist apartment block high on Highgate Hill, overlooking Kenwood. Here, at Highpoint, in a fourth floor eyrie with views twenty miles distant, north and south, Susan was nursed devotedly by Geoffrey through her closing months in 1986.

'Back I went to the drawing board', Jellicoe then wrote to a sympathiser who had known him since childhood, and it is here that Susan remains alive in the deep subconscious.

Now, the links forged earlier with his niece Ann Jellicoe, playwright and author of *The Knack,* Roger Mayne, her husband, and their children, came to greater fruition in an extended family.

CHAPTER 8
ITALY REVISITED:
AN INDIAN SUMMER

'Vital traditions of the past. . .permissibly and valuably overlaid with the stringent realities of modern Italian life'

The commission for a landscaped urban park for the city of Modena in northern Italy came to Geoffrey Jellicoe in 1980, soon after work had begun on designing the scheme for Sutton Place. Moreover, while Sutton Place had been designed with the individual subconscious mind in evidence, Modena came to represent for Jellicoe that which was most relevant to the collective mind as described by Jung. For at Modena many strands of Jellicoe's own life and experience seemed to come together.

As one whose sensibilities towards the design of landscape gardens had first truly been awakened in Italy, he was now able to work in one of her finest medieval cities where the vital traditions of the past could still be permissibly yet valuably overlaid with the stringent realities of modern Italian life. For Modena, the Commune is everything to stand and fight for, even to the extent of a locally elected Communist Party. Here Jellicoe found a very different set of precepts and constraints from those evident at Sutton Place, yet no less substantial and as enlightened in aspiration. On the one hand there was inspired Texan capitalism, of the kind that moves mountains; on the other classical, grassroots socialism, tempered by the agrarian idealism of Antonio Gramsci.[1] But such oppositions, Jellicoe feels, can be fully reconciled by the universal application of the art of landscape design.

If the environments that humanity struggles to create are a projection of the human psyche, whether individual or collective, the consequence can be the reduction or dispersion of such disruption or disharmony that occurs through the repression of man's subconscious instincts. Jellicoe believed increasingly that this reality lay at the basis of the art of landscape, whether the project in hand was a garden, a town, or even a whole region: the basis had to be the same. Never before had the opportunity occurred to test out such intangible yet pressing concepts. He realised, drawing again on his own past, that what Modena needed, within the city on the derelict, fallow site proposed, was a hymn to the countryside — inside the city, and his early training in classical Latin enabled him to recall the soft rhythms of Virgil, who wrote:

> Yet if I cannot reach these distant realms of nature because of some cold spiritless blood around my heart, then let me love the country, the rivers running through valleys, the streams and woodlands — happy though unknown. Give me broad fields and sweeping rivers, lofty mountain ranges in distant lands, cold precipitous valleys, where I may lie beneath the enormous darkness of the branches![2]

1 Antonio Gramsci (1891-1937) was a prominent Italian socialist of Sicilian origin who was imprisoned by Mussolini and whose ideas of practical social development sprang into prominence following the devaluation of communism and its moral collapse in the 1950s. These ideas sprang from an agrarian basis, reflecting Gramsci's own roots in agriculturally backward Sicily.
2 Virgil, *The Georgics*, 2482-90.

Modena today is a prosperous city with an economy largely based on industry, and famous as the home of Ferrari cars. But the history of this city of some 175,000 people has, like that of neighbouring Mantua, been as an agricultural centre. In Roman times the Via Emilia linked the city with the rest of Italy — Milan to the north, Rome to the south, while a series of ancient canals, also part of an irrigation network for the surrounding fields, linked Modena to the sea. The city's core is still dominated by a romanesque campanile which overlooks a centre wholly medieval in plan, within which the predominant architecture is that of the Italian Renaissance, rich with numerous arcades and squares.

Under the new plans for Modena, prepared by the distinguished architect and town planner Leonardo Benevolo, the proposed park has been sited as close to the centre as possible. And Jellicoe knew, from the works of the painter Giorgio di Chirico, typified by 'The Mystery and Melancholy of the Street' (1914), the need that northern Italian cities have for places of contemplation and reflection. The cities turn inwards, as in di Chirico's surrealist renderings, offering only the shuttered empty streets of noonday or midnight, of desolation and loneliness in sharp contrast to the feverish activity of working hours. Jellicoe considers that what is required is an antidote, a total reversal of known assumptions, and thus absolutely characteristic of Virgil's own ordering of priorities. For Virgil, too, reversed the accepted order, summoning nature to enable urbanity to survive. Nowhere other than in Virgil does the country expand into the city, and he clung to the agrarian ordering of work and leisure:

> But happy too the man who knows the goods of the country,
> Pan, old Silvanus, and the sister Nymphs.
> Unmoved by the power of the people, the crown and robes of monarchs...
> Fruit offered by the branches, and the generous crops freely borne by the soil,
> he can enjoy.
> He knows not iron-bound laws, insane mobs, records of state.[3]

For his part, Jellicoe quotes from E M Forster:

> The art of Virgil seems the wrong way up — if we assume the art of Homer
> is the right way up. He loves most the things that profess to matter least —
> a simile rather than the action it illustrates, a city full of apple trees rather
> than the soldiers who march out of it.[4]

In Modena the arcades and piazzas strive to accommodate various objects related to each other in space, within an evident hierarchy of urbanised pedestrian spaces each holding special significance greater in degree to that offered by the objects themselves. Jellicoe claims that in such a manner the proposed city park must complement these local characteristics, even expanding their importance in a way that Virgil would have enjoyed.

Firstly the city park has to be perceptibly part of the central core of the whole city. In its layout the park must become an evident analogy for the whole landscape surrounding the city within a plain through which the river Po runs, a perspective lengthened by the view of the distant Apennine mountains. In the park's microcosm, the country expands into the city, a reversal completed.

3 Ibid, 2493-8.
4 Quoted by Jellicoe in *Architectural Review*, 1033, March 1983, p49.

View of the city of Modena with the prominent campanile. Jellicoe's highpoints in the proposed urban park in Modena were an artificial hill and a tower, which would link and unite the twentieth century with the medieval town and campanile

Modena; the predominant architecture is that of the Italian Renaissance, rich with numerous arcades and squares. Jellicoe's proposals for the park complemented the local characteristics of architecture and space and recognised the way northern Italian cities turn in on themselves, with the shuttered sunlit streets of midday in sharp contrast to the feverish activity of working hours

Virgilian landscape, medieval townscape: much of Jellicoe's theory for the Modena project was based on Virgil's idea of summoning nature to enable urbanity to survive

The project is a form of homage to Virgil,[5] who was born not far away on a Mantuan farm in 70 BC. In the three major poems that collectively comprise Virgil's principle *oeuvre*, the *Eclogues* are predominantly pastoral, the *Georgics* are, by contrast, didactic and the *Aeneid* is a heroic consummation of human endeavour — a curiously modernist consummation, a fact which did not escape Jellicoe's eye. The relevance of Modena at a time when the modernist ethos was being called into question and subverted through the civic resurrection of the vocabulary of classical architecture, meant that for Jellicoe it was important to reassert the essential humanism of classical thought, not as a source for replication on the building envelope, but in reinforcing certain basic ideals. As such, Virgil's combination of a romantic engagement with the landscape (based on agrarian experience), coupled with a recognisable urbanity, best reflected and recharged the multi-layered Italian environment. In the *Eclogues,* the rigours, endeavour, and remaining sanctuaries of rural life are realistically deployed, without escapism. Jellicoe claims at Modena to place primary value upon the continuing mystique of nature. The design must be a projection of our human psyche, and visitors and locals alike should find the park to be drawing out a response from their human, inbuilt instincts in nature, which Jellicoe considers are normally repressed by urban conditions.

While Leonardo Benevolo's structure plan was based on abstract geometry (albeit echoing the man-made agricultural landscape patterns of the Po valley yet

5 For an insight into Jellicoe's study of Roman (Augustan) poets, *Poets in a Landscape,* Gilbert Highet, Pelican Books, 1959, provides a superbly clear description of the works of Virgil and others against their historical and geographical background. Jellicoe has frequently referred to Highet's work, now sadly long out of print.

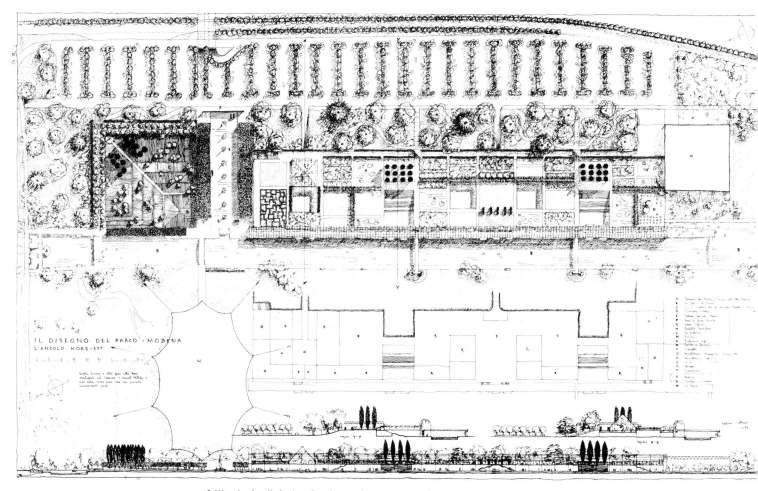

Jellicoe's detailed plan for the north-east corner of the city park, Modena, 1982

contrasting with the medieval centre), Jellicoe urged an introduction of such elements of English romantic landscape that would still strike a chord into the primary landscape of myth, illusion and enigma. By creating such highpoints as an artificial hill and a distant tower, park and city could be reunited. It was as though an outcrop of the Apennine foothills had materialised.

Here, too, a water feature, as in the majority of Jellicoe's constructs, constitutes a primary element, establishing also the main directional grid. Known as the Long Water, it runs the full length of the site. Along this we find a well-shaded, brick-paved piazza incorporating a water mill; next a pool for sculpture and an octave of musical fountains runs off at right angles, a sculptural wall terminating the pool; to one side there is a stage for impromptu theatre in the European tradition. Continuing in a southerly direction along the edge of the Long Water, other facilities include a tropical plant house, a lily pool, a swimming pool with sliding roof, restaurants, bars and cafés, while along the 330 metre long axis of the glass gallery are shops, offices and a museum. The whole was under an extensive botanical roof garden. The Long Water is crossed at four key points by bridges. For those wishing to experience a special mystery in entering this complex, it is possible to enter from the north, via a grotto of the underworld, so reaching the water terrace directly.

Such a scheme is a statement about the essential identity of Modena. The economy of the city is increasingly dependent upon industry but it is a series of agricultural canals, also part of an irrigational system, that link Modena to the sea, and by imitating these in his proposals Jellicoe has distilled the whole essence of the community and its history in the formation of the park.

The project remains in abeyance as political power changes hands between different groups in the maelstrom of northern Italian politics. And Jellicoe, too, has moved on, although the project could be implemented at anytime.

Another Italian commission, Brescia, like that at Modena, came through Leonardo Benevolo and Jellicoe's project exploited the steep site and the possibility of an elaborate system of water.

Brescia is a Lombardian city on the edge of the Alps. Jellicoe had only a brief stay there and little time in which to consider a scheme. Within the area to be considered lay a farm suggesting the time of Vignola, still complete, and, thought Jellicoe, exemplary enough to be worth preserving. This was an ideal element in what was to be a public park. In his description of Brescia in *The Landscape of Man,* Jellicoe argued the case:

> The potential field for creative design is as infinite as its sources are unpredictable and sometimes grotesque. It was a chance supper [given by his hosts at Brescia] of five different kinds of fresh fish from Lake Isoe, one after another, that inspired the 'infilling' landscape project for the estate at Brescia beside the foothills of the Alps. To combat the rigidity of the architecture, fishes drawn from the adjoining water landscape now metamorphosed into artificial hills, split the two parts of the estate, linking *en route* not only the usual pleasures of parkland, but a live farm and a cemetery to complete the cycle of life.

The commune, however, seemed not to be amused, and it proved an abortive project, however, despite Jellicoe's enthusiastic presentation in so short a period of gestation.

Jellicoe had Ovid very much in mind when he developed the concept of the 'fishes' at Brescia. The Roman poet (b43BC) produced his famous work *Metamorphoses* as a collection of myths. This superb work has been quarried by writers and artists for the source of numerous poems, songs, allegories and fables. The poem asserts that neither gods nor men live life to any particular plan, pursuing it through their passions alone. Ovid reveals stories from the Aeneid, as Gilbert Highet says: 'making them more exciting, less meaningful, shallower and more vivid, occasionally almost comic'.[6]

After Brescia, Italy receded from Jellicoe's immediate preoccupations, but in 1985 *Italian Gardens of the Renaissance* was seized upon by an English-based architectural publisher who invited Jellicoe to write a fresh introduction, and in this he wrote of

> ...the Villa Gamberaia where a landscape in its own right seemed to express all the facets of the human mind. It is a period I have found of inexhaustible interest. If you can paint a portrait of the human mind in landscape does not this ease the tensions within that mind!

6 *Poets in a Landscape,* see 5 above, p183.

Typical urban environment with high density housing close to the site where Brescia's urban park was planned

Ancient farmland within the Brescia proposed urban park site

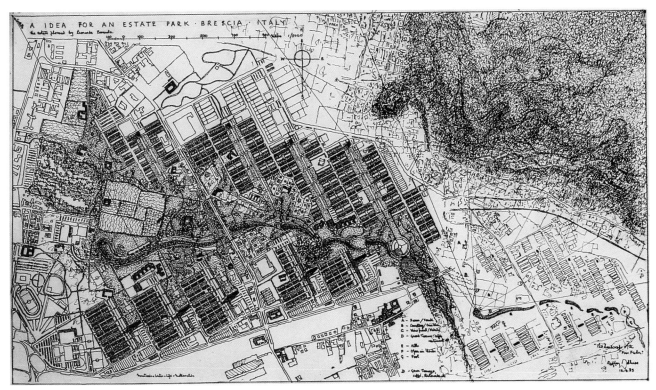

Jellicoe's plan for Brescia's proposed urban park exploited the steep site and included an elaborate water system

Jellicoe dedicated the introduction to the memory of Jock Shepherd, his co-author, who had died in 1978, for the return to Italy and the involvement with Modena and Brescia had rekindled old memories. But after the three or so years that were to follow this soliloquy, devoted solely to schemes for the Moody Gardens, Galveston (the subject of the next chapter), Jellicoe again felt the frustration of postponement.

While on the one hand he would look forward, as so often in the past, to a period for the intake of knowledge, a time of research during which the batteries could, so to speak, be recharged, on the other hand he found the necessarily long delay before execution of the Moody Gardens project in 1993 had become not only a test of his resolve, but also of his health.

Although an oasis of welcome relief remained at Shute to mediate the long hours and days spent on the Galveston drawings, Jellicoe worked on alone, in the small, glass-block walled re-entrant inside his Highpoint flat. But in early 1988 Jellicoe's wing of the apartment block was suddenly enclosed in polythene cladding. Feeling like the inhabitant of a Christo project,[7] Jellicoe worked on regardless while essential remedial work was carried out to the building. After a few weeks, by mid-March, his health began to fail.

At this juncture he was persuaded by friends to leave for a while and he took the train to Scotland to recuperate in a small cottage protected by woods and overlooking the North Sea. Here, after three days, he made a remarkable recovery, and was soon sketching by the wood fire, talking animatedly and, above all, humorously reminiscing to his hosts. He had recovered, but it had been a salutary reminder in time.

Soon afterwards, he made a further visit to the country, this time to Shute, where the laboratory of ideas remained intact. A relief to the later days of the

7 Christo, the American artist, flourished in the context of growing social awareness of environmental issues in the 1970s and 1980s. His symbolic and literal 'wrapping' of major landscape features as well as buildings in plastic sheeting became famous.

153

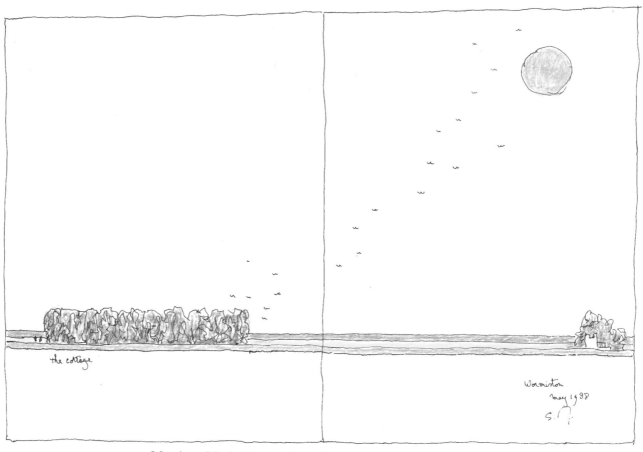

Wormiston Wood, Fife: Geoffrey Jellicoe's drawing in Scotland illustrates his fundamental reaction to landscape, in which the initial response is simple and straightforward

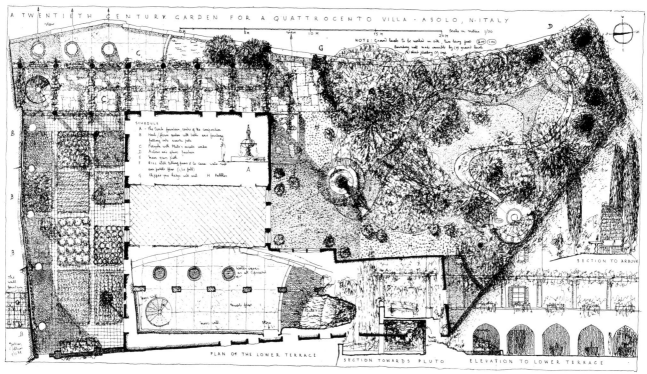

At Asolo, Jellicoe once again relied on the element of water, deploying it in various forms, including a rill, and culminating in the grand fountain (A) in the centre of the scheme

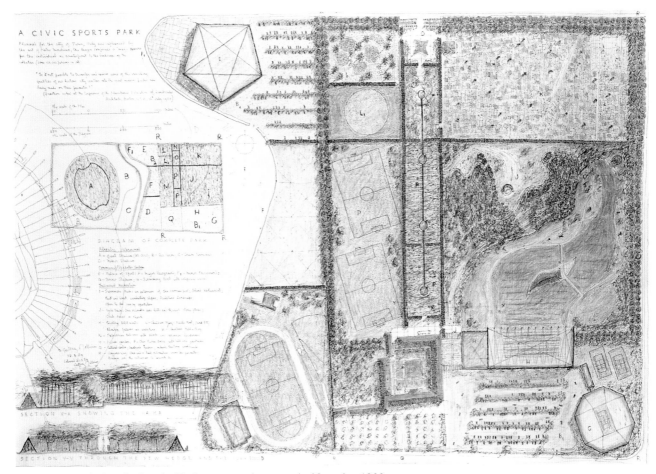

Jellicoe was invited to develop the Turin sports park concept in November 1988

Moody Gardens design came in the finalising of that for Shute, including a new woodland garden inspired by Lady Anne Tree which he could develop in the sure knowledge that, as with everything at Shute, execution of the works would not be delayed more than a season.

Working on Shute again, Jellicoe's pace of mind quickened. Further encouraged by the accolade received in the summer of 1988 at Boston at the annual gathering of the International Federation of Landscape Architects, he felt ready for the arrival of two further projects which arrived within one month of each other. Both were from Italy.

The death of the Italian landscape designer Pietro Porcinai of Florence had led his family to contact Jellicoe to write a tribute to an old colleague for a publication. Porcinai had executed a project at Asolo, a small medieval township on the foothills of the Dolomites sixty miles north of Venice. Now, suddenly, there arrived from a former client a commission to design a twentieth century garden for a quattrocento villa at Asolo. Flying to Venice in the late autumn of 1988, there was a noticeable spring in his step.

Within a few days of receiving the commission the scheme was drawn up in Highgate. On the one hand the proposal is a restatement of quattrocento formalism appropriate to such a villa, with terraces, formal beds for herbs and other practicalities deemed essential; and on the other hand it contains an evocation of the necessary psyche of twentieth century man. An arbour (for repose

Geoffrey Jellicoe at work on the Turin sports park proposals in 1990. The Mondrian square can be clearly seen to the right of the drawing

and vista) looks back towards a great new fountain, and across towards a second arbour set on a lower plane. Linking two water courses is a rill which runs down over rounded pebbles through a cool and shady bosco within a wholly secluded enclave. Below the villa itself, and at the end of a marbled terrace edged by a moss wall, lies Pluto's cavern. Privacy is paramount.

The villa is ancient, and surrounded by the village it once commanded. The usual sounds of Italian communal activity percolate everywhere: church bells, the games of children, two-stroke engines and barking dogs. But Jellicoe mutes the background noise by means of the soft trickle of rill and fountain.

The second call from Italy for Jellicoe's attention came from Turin. The city was planning a new sports park next to a stadium already under construction. The project was an exciting venture and followed hard on the heels of the Asolo scheme. On 22 November 1988 Jellicoe flew to Turin, returning three days later, and by 5 December the project was already designed in considerable detail.

At the Boston conference Jellicoe had thrown to the audience a quotation from a letter to the British Institute's journal: 'Could not the modern park, for instance, fill the metaphysical void once filled by church and cathedral?'

Unlike that for Modena, the Turin park had a brief that was almost totally sports related. However, the existing and typically spacious farmhouse was to be retained as a cultural centre. Jellicoe developed a metaphysical square in his concept, asking himself:

> Is it possible to transfer the metaphysics of an historic city centre to a modern collective park? The internal Mondrian-inspired proportions are defined by four metre high clipped hedges. A stately landscape gallery, possibly of fountains, leads to the cultural heart of the project.

Much of Jellicoe's vision crystallised from the air.

> On leaving Turin airport on a beautifully clear November day, we circled the city with its neighbouring Alps. We passed over the site and I saw clearly the whole concept of this mighty stadium oval in its grid-iron of streets and (very important) the adjoining River Po with its islands. This view justifies the placing of a romantic lake landscape within the Mondrian square.

Once again, Jellicoe had responded with alacrity to the Italian initiatives, drawing deeply upon his reservoir of familiarity with the Italian landscape and its varied topography. To this sure foundation was fused his intuitive realisation of the central thrust of European culture in the twentieth century, as epitomised by the works of the Dutch master Piet Mondrian. What could be more appropriate, in the flat region of Turin, than these spatial concepts that would unite horizon and sky in a linear perspective so implanted in this great landscape that otherwise was prone to fragmentation and visual fracturing through the urban extensions of the city of Turin? The designer's debt to Italy could well be repaid.

The Island of Galveston, Texas. The challenge of the site was there: wetlands battered by climate, as if suspended on the edge of the known world; in reality an abandoned wartime airfield on the shore of the Gulf of Mexico

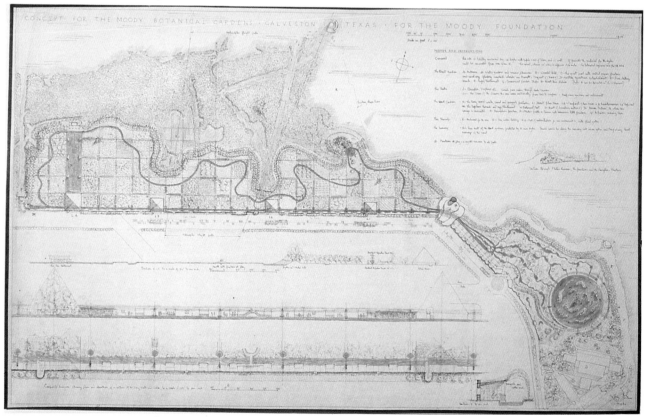

The initial design concept, 1984

CHAPTER 9
THE SINGLE GRAND IDEA:
THE MOODY GARDENS

'The fullest possible explanation of landscape history'

In 1983, following completion of the designs for Sutton Place, Geoffrey Jellicoe at last felt able to consider other work. A young botanist, Peter Atkins, made contact with him. Atkins had himself been entrusted with an appealing task by the Moody Foundation of Galveston, Texas. He had been funded to undertake a six month study period at Kew. His own brief had been agreed beforehand. He was to undertake a scheme for the layout of a botanical garden on the island of Galveston, adjoining an abandoned airfield and its wild hinterland of wetlands.

At the time, Jellicoe had no wish whatever to work in Texas, and for some six months or so he refused Atkins, but the botanist was persistent, and eventually Jellicoe agreed, in 1984, to travel out to Houston and from there to make his way out to the island of Galveston to view the site. Although the barren expanse looked forbidding, Jellicoe was intrigued.

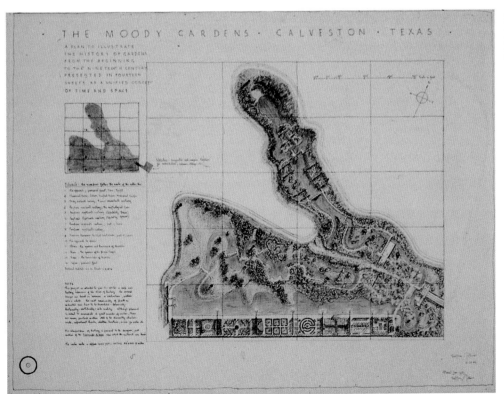

The final scheme for the Moody Historical Gardens as conceived and drawn by Geoffrey Jellicoe

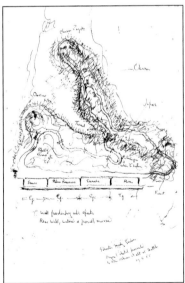

The revised concept for the Moody Gardens as conceived overnight and revealed by Jellicoe at Seattle to Moody representatives in May 1985. It appears to be a remarkably accurate preliminary to the final scheme

With Galveston, Geoffrey Jellicoe recognised a challenge. If he could pull it off here, he felt, and given the budget and the necessary will on the part of the foundation, he could establish a masterpiece of twentieth century landscape design that would incorporate an ecological and botanical perspective within a major work of landscape art. He was on.

The subsequent terms of reference given to him at this point were fairly broad and within an overall budget of some thirty million dollars, as well as an annual operational target of not more than one and a half million dollars at 1985 prices.

The island of Galveston nestles close in to the coast of Texas. In 1900 it contained a prosperous city that was suddenly all but annihilated by a massive inundation in which some six thousand people were lost. Today it is again a successful community, secure now behind a massive sea wall. The island is some thirty miles long, and on average some two miles wide. The seawall runs for ten and a half miles and is fifteen feet high. Thus Seawall Boulevard had been created, and runs its full length as a four lane seaside thoroughfare. At the south end of this the route leads on to the wetlands beyond, and the adjoining airfield site.

Galveston's population runs close to seventy thousand, but the proximity of the city of Houston swells this throughout the holiday period. Even after summer's 'golden months' there comes an illusion of stability and natural equilibrium: great sea shells lie unheeded on the clean sands, while cranes, wild geese and duck migrate in overhead and settle in the wetlands.

But it is a false sense of security. Nature in the Gulf of Mexico is volatile with extremes of temperature and the salt content in the air can retard plant growth drastically. Perhaps it was to address this challenge and surmount it in a truly Texan manner that the Moody Foundation decided to approach Jellicoe with the commission for a design to provide an ambitious and superlative set of gardens such as has never previously existed in the history of landscape design.

Galveston as a leisure and domestic environment does not lack for supporters. In the mid-1980s, a New York-based survey comparing American cities rated Galveston '12th Best Place to Live in the USA', out of 277 such cities, while New York City rated 156th.

Yet such a project as the Moody Gardens seems implausible, a wild fantasy. The wetlands appear to hang on the edge of the known world. From the air, this expanse of flat oblivion offers only the negation of life. These 126 acres are bounded by the ocean on one side. On the other lies the airfield and its abandoned sections in the form of a disused runway and some curiously triangulated canals with, more usefully, a service road running the full length of the site. There are also two existing flight paths serving the operational airport itself, limiting building potential and accepting a flight density of up to fifty planes per day. Conditions are hardly ideal.

With confidence in his own skills, and a lifetime of design experience to draw upon, Jellicoe was far from dismayed. He addressed himself with a sense of urgency to this massive direction of material wealth to the empty expanse of wetlands. Here close to the end of his working life, he had been presented with the opportunity to create a landscape design of unprecedented significance.

In his first proposal of April 1984, Jellicoe reached for 'majesty, drama, and singleness of purpose'. 'It would have been the grandest landscape in the modern world', as he put it at the time. Yet in what manner does the designer communicate such a grand plan to the average visitor as he wanders through it? This, Jellicoe found, was the dilemma. He believes today that this can only be achieved by reaching the individual subconscious mind. It is not a theme park. 'Like a grand opera. . .there must be a sense of having been through an experience that is greater than life. . .like a grand opera'. This must be achieved by the symbolism of the landscape and the way in which it finds its way subliminally to the unconscious mind.

The concept for this first scheme is of major relevance in any understanding of Jellicoe's work, since it essentially forms the third and final element in what he considered to be a trilogy, three consecutive projects which he referred to at the time as his 'Augustan poets' series. The series of landscapes was founded upon the works of Virgil, Ovid and Lucretius. Modena related naturally to the works of Virgil. Brescia harked back to Ovid. Now, as at Sutton Place, Jellicoe turned readily to Lucretius. Galveston provided a context within which the lengthy Lucretian work *De Rerum Natura* provided a message that struck at the very basis of human life and its place in nature.

Jellicoe was aware of the growing apprehension in the 1980s concerning the survival both of man and of nature. With Epicurean guile and elegantly persuasive verse, Lucretius set out in his great work to draw humanity back to its origins, abandoning the accumulated superstitions and prejudices which confused these basic truths. As he wrote:

> This dread and darkness of the mind cannot be dispelled by the sunbeams, the shining shafts of day, but only by an understanding of the outward form and inner workings of nature.[1]

Jellicoe grasped this central concept. There had to be a single purpose here, the provision within a single primary idea, of a garden of plants, not in any way related to humanity as such. This essential, primary idea accordingly had to accommodate, as Jellicoe put it:

> The terryifying forces of nature. . .the creation of haven for plant life in the midst of chaos, and the work of man to preserve this life by protecting walls, water, soil, and service paths. There is no human history here, only that of the plant and the assembly of species from all over the entire globe.[2]

Contrasting with the surrounding wastelands and the ravages of the Gulf of Mexico against these wetlands, the Moody Botanical Gardens would provide a scientific exposition of natural botanical evolution, laid out in a pattern of rhythmic spaces with the same cohesion and harmony as a musical score. On the periphery the sea would even be permitted to reclaim some of the wetland areas: at this point the Sea Restaurant would stand, perched on the partly submerged promontory to the north of the site, and only accessible by boat. It would stand, so to speak, on the edge of the known world.

The entire site was to be enclosed by a dyke some fifteen feet high. Along this

1 *De Rerum Natura*, Lucretius, II, pp144-7.
2 'The Triumph of Jellicoe', E M Farrell, *Architectural Review*, 1063, September 1985, p9.

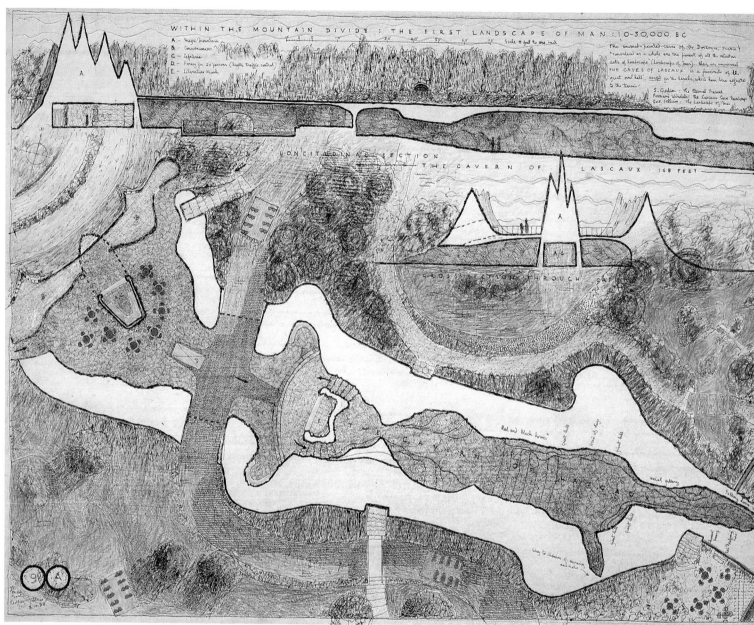

Within the Mountain Divide, on the top of the drawing, handwritten:

WITHIN THE MOUNTAIN DIVIDE : THE FIRST LANDSCAPE OF MAN : 10-30,000 BC

A – Magic Mountain
B – Conveniences
C – Cafeteria
D – Ferry for 30 person (lights traffic control)
E – Literature Kiosk

The animal-painted-caves of the Dordogne, France, considered as a whole are the parent of all the intuitive arts of landscape ('Landscape of man'). they are unrivalled. THE CAVES OF LASCAUX is a facsimile of the 'great oval hall', except for the levels, which have been adjusted to the terrain.

S. Giedion : the Eternal Present
Fernand Windels: the Lascaux Cave Paintings
G.A. Jellicoe : the Landscape of man

LONGITUDINAL SECTION
THE CAVERN OF LASCAUX · 168 FEET

CROSS SECTION THROUGH GAP

Within the Mountain Divide, underneath the pinnacle of the Magic Mountain the first landscape of man is discovered: the great oval cavern of Lascaux a replica of the cavern location and its complex imagery from prehistory. Jellicoe has ingeniously contrived the perfect subject with which to create a further, underground dimension for the visitor. (Drawing of the final scheme)

would run a triple row of trees. The enclosed space would contain over fifty quarter-acre plots, each designed with special reference to the ecology and habitat of given species of plants.

Various leisure activities would be concentrated at the eastern end of the site, close to the entrance. From here the circuit begins.

The visitor would board a water-bus for the trip through the whole complex, quietly and stage by stage progressing down a long and arcaded water avenue, through water arches and past gargoyles, passing along the way four evenly spaced out glasshouses of pyramid form. Gradually the range, size and variety of botanical growth would increase the perception of the traveller, moving detachedly as through a non-human universe. And so the world perceived by Lucretius would emerge for man 'in' a botanical landscape of the universe. The theme is one of creation, growth, pollination and survival of species on the edge of chaos. The sea gives and the sea takes back. So was an Epicurean philosophy to be translated into

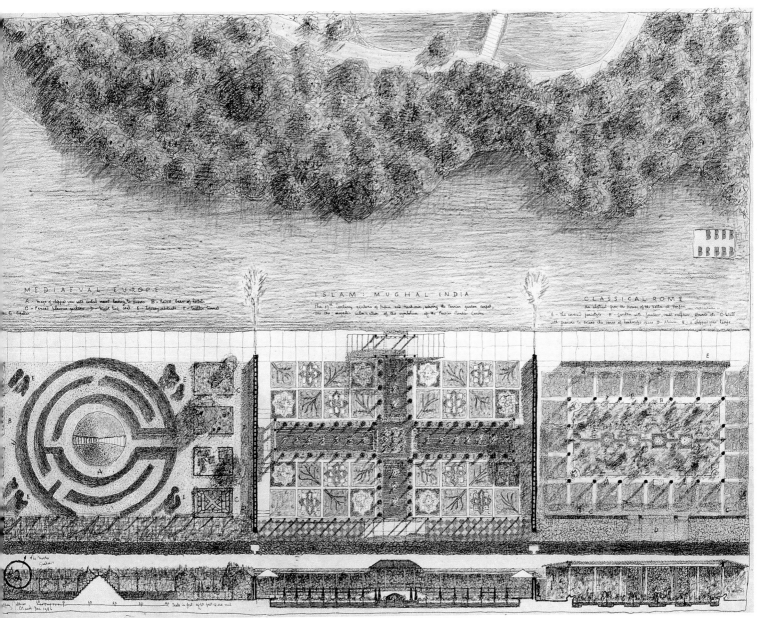

Within the drawing, the following inscribed labels appear:

MEDIAEVAL EUROPE

ISLAM: MUGHAL INDIA

CLASSICAL ROME

the art of landscape as a comprehensible, perceptible experience.

So in the single grand idea of the universe here contained, Jellicoe extrapolated a concept of the world as it might be. Between order and chaos he offered, in this first set of proposals, a twenty-first century world view of which human aspirations form a part, merging with the inspiration of the collective unconscious to beget the survival of all species.

In the final analysis it is this first scheme (see page 158) for the Moody Foundation which surely must be Jellicoe's finest epitaph, a distillation which he proposes will take the art of landscape forward into the third millennium. Nor are historical references, allegories or myths required where science and the knowledge of plants are themselves explicit about the essence of life and its ensuing ecologies. The purity of this idea stands as his witness. The symphony, although scored in draft, for the most part in 1984, will never be performed. Yet it remains, so to speak, the great unfinished symphony of landscape today.

Medieval Europe, Islam/Mughal India, Classical Rome. Here Jellicoe reveals the delights of the formalised garden as developed in Classical Rome. AD 79 marks the period of the house of the Vettii, here paraphrased together with (centre) the parallel and later developments in Mughal India. Later the medieval garden emerged with the symbolism that continues to interest Jellicoe today. (Drawing of the final scheme)

163

In our mind's eye, the return journey winds back along a less formalised route than before, the water-bus threads its way lazily through the great open botanical plantings with their orderly gridding. The Texan sun is deflected by the canopy over the boat: now and then we remain aware of an aircraft passing overhead, and of the movement of the sea against the fifteen foot high man-made barrier of the dyke guarding the periphery.

The problem was that the botanical gardens in themselves, as originally conceived by the Moody Foundation, would never generate enough income from admissions to establish basic feasibility.

In later discussions, when the whole saga of Galveston had been completed, and the drawings fully documented for the second full proposal, Jellicoe would draw on the written work of a number of authors, using passages of prose almost like a tuning fork, testing out relevances. For instance, there is a compelling passage in V S Naipaul's *The Enigma of Arrival*. Naipaul's figure describes a journey made between first coming and actual arrival. After many tribulations and some fear and confusion, the visitor:

> . . .would come upon a door, open it, and find himself back on the quayside of arrival. He has been saved; the world is as he remembered it. Only one thing is missing now. Above the cut-out walls and buildings there is no mast, no sail. The antique ship has gone. The traveller has lived out his life.[3]

For Jellicoe, the end of the journey must signify arrival, rather than any ending. There must have been a sense of revelation. The world cannot just be as one remembered it. Life must have been enriched by its very passage, individually and collectively.

The influence of Jung grew perceptibly as a force within Jellicoe's thinking as the Galveston project continued. Between the first proposal and the last, he felt increasingly concerned over what Jung has referred to as 'loss of soul' in man. How, Jellicoe wondered, could one reconcile the Lucretian ideal with the growth of scientific materialism? Where was the spirit of man as the twentieth century approached its final decade? In Jung's view it could at least be verified through the working hypothesis of the collective unconscious.

Such thoughts assisted Jellicoe in moving forward from this first proposal, that of 1984, through to the 1985 scheme which has become the basis of the present proposals. The project now is much smaller than its precursor, and rather more complicated, the fruit of compromise at many stages. At one point he had claimed that it was not really comparable in grandeur. Appendix III is an extract of an article by Jellicoe on the Historical Gardens of the Moody Foundation, as they came to be known.

With a view to securing a sound degree of financial self-sufficiency the brief was now amended to include an hotel, a theatre, an expanded educational facility, and a form of nursery for the study of plant growth and research facilities and linked to the ecology of the remaining wetlands. Much of the initial Lucretian influence remained, but the necessity of providing a major theme that would further attract visitors on an increasing scale led to the decision to incorporate what Jellicoe called

3 *The Enigma of Arrival*, V S Naipaul, Penguin, 1987, p92.

'The Landscape of Civilisation as Experienced in The Moody Historical Gardens'. The metamorphosis was dramatic. *The Landscape of Man* had, of course, been published by Geoffrey and Susan Jellicoe in 1975, and as a primary text proved an instant success. This now became the basis for the Moody Historical Gardens, which balanced developments between western and eastern civilisations over the centuries. In May 1985 Jellicoe produced, in a hotel bedroom in Seattle where he was staying at the time, the basic idea in sketch form. Over the next three years he refined the project in every detail drawing effortlessly upon his historical knowledge and experience.

Instantly Jellicoe seemed to have adjusted to the necessary reality that the project must be operationally self-financing. The result is one which exploits the romantic/classical difference in landscape thinking and the contrast between romantic and secular landscapes, mainly from France, England and Russia, with the more spiritual gardens and landscapes created in China and Japan. By way of contrast the classical landscapes, ranging from Persia through the Italian Renaissance and beyond, complete the picture. Over four so-called primeval cultures Jellicoe accordingly laid twelve civilisations. The gardens were intended to remain true to the original ideal of expressing the ultimate unity of all existence. As Anthony Storr writes:

> Jung's belief in the ultimate unity of all existence led him to suppose that physical and mental as well as spatial and temporal were human categories imposed upon reality which did not accurately reflect it.[4]

Jellicoe liked also to quote from the collected works of Jung:

> For indeed our consciousness does not create itself — it wells up from unknown depths. In childhood it awakens gradually, and all through life it wakes each morning out of the depths of sleep from an unconscious condition.[5]

Throughout the aftermath of the Galveston presentation, in 1986 and 1987, and during the painstaking production of the detailed drawings, Jellicoe continued to amend and refine the scheme. Resigned now to the eventuality of never himself seeing the finished project, let alone perhaps even a start, he has continued to believe that the best guarantee of progress in that direction would be through ensuring the widest possible public and professional awareness of the project.

One important amendment derived from his continuing exploration of the workings of the human subconscious, searching out the roots of superstition, and the impulses that breed romanticism, rather than sweeping these emotions and feelings away in a grand Epicurean gesture. As a result, the caves at Lascaux were now inserted in replica form (see page 162). This flashback to the earliest mental landscapes of man coincided with Jellicoe's re-reading of Jung. Subsequent recourse to Thomas Mann's masterpiece, *The Magic Mountain*, led to some rethinking of the space allocated hitherto to the Mughal Garden, which re-emerged as 'the case for the Magic Mountain'.

Further revisions were made to the western classical sequence: Eden, was now characterised by the addition of the symbolic apple crowning a bend in the canal.

4 *Jung: Selected Writings*, edited by Anthony Storr, Fontana, 1983.
5 *Psychology and Religion: West and East*, C G Jung, collected works 11, pp567ff.

165

European Eighteenth Century. Here Jellicoe represents the dichotomy of Classical and Romantic as articulated in eighteenth century France. The Petit Trianon and the fetishes of Versailles are reached only after the water-bus has swept past a romantic landscape that evokes in its contrived drama the world of Salvator Rosa. (Drawings here and opposite of the final scheme)

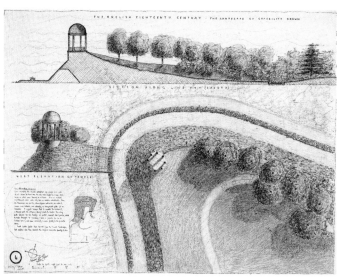

The English Eighteenth Century. Capability Brown seemed eminently appropriate as a representative of this period when purism overtook English predilections, and Jellicoe obeys the rules by removing any public access other than via the water-bus and its passage past the Belvedere; only deer may roam across these arcadian pastures

166

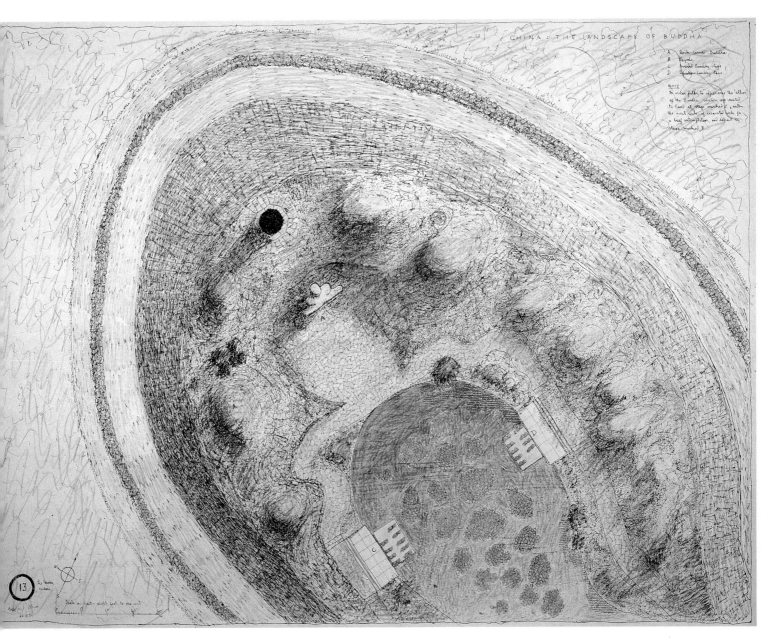

Provision was made nearby for small groups of wild animals; viewing balconies were added. A prehistoric burial mound was designated within the primeval forest. In the Italian Renaissance garden, an old friend, the monster of Bomarzo, was imported to fill a void and, while alarming adults, to attract children. A bronze head of Poseidon has been successfully modelled by the British sculptor Keith McCarter, to be located close to water trumpets on the walls at the classical division. A constant refinement was pursued, and the whole scheme embellished further into 1988 and beyond.

The water-buses themselves seem to convey a childlike sense of wonderment, as they appear in the drawings, meandering from one landscape vignette to another, and assist the viewer of the drawings in relating to scale and content. They possess a curiously typical condition of buoyant jollity, perhaps no less than a reflection of Jellicoe's own ultimate confidence in the achievement of the whole project.

For this indeed is Jellicoe's exegesis, his achievement and the fullest possible explanation of landscape history, ecology and survival.

To Jellicoe, the emergence of Buddha in this Chinese sanctuary is one of the most important events in the sequence, and the water-bus moors in placid waters. This is possibly the greatest of Jellicoe's Moody drawings, and seems wholly of the twentieth century, reading like an isolated moonshot or frame-up from a helicopter. Vegetation seems to have been freeze dried and there is an absolute obligation to disembark, the only instance in the sequence when such a ritual must be observed

167

CHAPTER 10
THE CONTRIBUTION TO THEORY

'The importance of the solace of landscape is only gradually being recognised as of primary significance, over and above other elements in the built environment. It is the battle of recognition that Jellicoe has set himself to win'

As the third millennium steals upon the world, architects and landscape architects alike might well echo Leonardo da Vinci whose rhetorical poser still stands like a cautionary beacon: 'Dimmi se mai fit fatto alcuna cosa?' (Tell me if anything was ever done?) This plea still reverberates across the centuries as it did over Leonardo's pages of observation and calculation. For Jellicoe, who shelved retirement in the early 1980s, the quest for a meaningful theoretical basis for landscape architecture has held a central role in his ordering of priorities. The frustrations of the post-war years seemed never ending, and only as a result of the opportunities brought in the 1980s have the art and science of landscape seemed reconcilable in terms of a broader philosophy. Jellicoe views the human predicament as one where nonetheless a lack of philosophical enlightenment is made all the more restrictive through the pressures of an essentially consumer and materialistic society.

On his own admission, he is no scientist; and he views the future of landscape architecture as inherently bound together with the creative development of humanity in the visual arts. Turning back upon architecture, he quoted (at the 1988 IFLA Boston Conference) Juhani Pallasmaa, a prominent architect thinker of today:

> The fundamental message of architecture is the very best existential expression: how does it feel to be human in this world? and the task of architecture is to make us experience our existence with deeper significance and purpose. Architecture is to make us know and remember who we are.[1]

The modern movement through most of the twentieth century had, however, little time for landscape considerations. Despite the search of architects of the Arts and Crafts movement for garden design that bore out such principles, modernists were for the most part happy to extend the legacy of the eighteenth century in accepting the programmatic and functional separation of architecture (buildings) from their surroundings (landscape).

There were notable examples to the contrary. Frank Lloyd Wright was unequivocal: the ground was more important than anything man would make out of it or put on it.[2] For Alvar Aalto, too, environmental considerations were paramount.[3] Both Wright and Aalto upheld a preoccupation with landscape as setting, enlivened by the symbolism of nature as form.

1 'Tradition and Modernity: The Feasbility of Regional Architecture in Post-Modern Society', Juhani Pallasmaa, *Architectural Review*, May 1988, pp26-34.
2 Quoted from *Frank Lloyd Wright and Nature*, Donald Hoffman, Dover, 1987, p3.
3 'It was Mantegna's painting that made me analyse the topography of Finnish towns. We also have hills, which are sometimes reminiscent of the holy land of Tuscany...the houses mount the slopes in terraces', Alvar Aalto papers, text of 1926, cf *Modern Times: Alvar Aalto, the Decisive Years*, Göran Schildt, Helsinki, 1986.

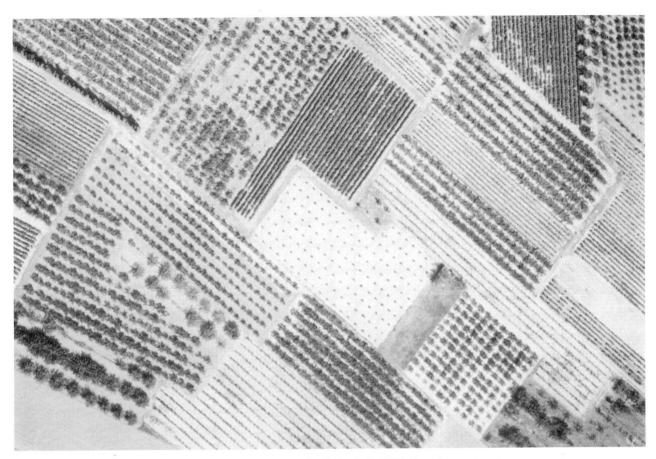

Thermographic print of orchards in the Avignon area of France. Le Corbusier's 'fifth' dimension — that of the aerial view — created the problem of reconciling the overview with the view at ground level. Jellicoe was deeply influenced by such theories and the composite vision it engendered in his approach to landscaping. From Les Immatériaux *by J-F Lyotard, 1985*

Le Corbusier's earliest works reveal a desire to incorporate traditional 'enlightenment' principles of landscape within a wholly contemporary idiom. The symbolic dimension of landscape space was never denied. Ultimately it seems he moved towards a full and parallel reconciliation of building and setting. At Chandigarh,[4] and most specifically in the disposition of spaces between the unexecuted Governor's Palace, its garden, and the Capitol complex, such aspirations were to be fulfilled as never before. 'The site', Le Corbusier would say to architectural students, 'is the nourishment offered by our eyes to our senses, to our intelligence, to our hearts. The site is the base of architectural composition'.[5]

Early in his work, Le Corbusier succeeded in isolating landscape from the built form, without reconciling the two. In the roof garden for the Beistegui roof terrace over the Champs Elysées in Paris (1931)[6] the garden symbolised a finite landscape form, with nature domesticated in a surrealist mode — appropriately for the period: far above street level, mythology was preserved intact.

Le Corbusier's vision of space was to be deeply extended in perception by the advent of aerial photography and the resultant aerial view. He even devoted a

4 *Oeuvre Complète 1957-1965,* Le Corbusier, Zurich, 1965.
5 *Le Corbusier Talks with Students,* Le Corbusier, trans Pierre Chase, New York, 1961, pp40-1.
6 *Le Corbusier: Urbanism, Algiers and Other Buildings and Projects, 1930-33,* Manfredo Tafuri, trans Stephen Sartarelli, New York, London and Paris, 1983, pp31-46.

A photograph of the Roman Forum, the Colosseum and the Arch of Constantine, Rome, taken in 1908. At this time Europeans were becoming aware of a new dimension and realising the impact of aerial photography on the view of landscape. From Giacomo Balla *by V D Dorazio, 1969*

whole volume[7] to the impact of flight, its machines, and its perceptions in the context of revolutionary change. The problem created by this 'fifth' dimension, as he called it, lay in the reconciliation of such overviews with the moving viewpoint at ground level. This was more than the effect of cubism and the composite vision it engendered. Yet in reality, the impact of this dramatically extended vision had little bearing upon most of the architecture.

In the ninteenth century, painting had come to be predominantly influenced by the mode of the 'typical' — what characteristics were typical more or less had to

7 *Aircraft,* Studio Publications, London, 1935.

170

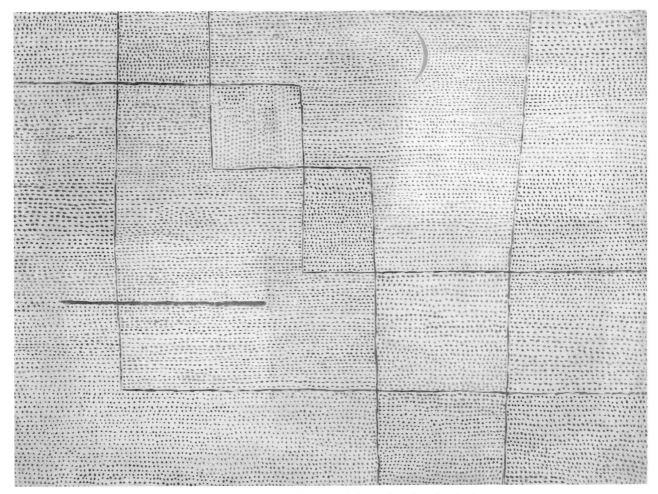

'Klarung' (Clarification), Paul Klee, 1932. A painting with close affinity to the print of orchards near Avignon (page 169) illustrates the influence which Klee had on Jellicoe's approach to landscape through careful gradations of scale and detail

be restated as such as a prerequisite in discovery. This convention ran parallel to the emergence of the idea of organic evolution in science. The synonymous abandonment of classical ideas about order opened up the possibility of a system based on the scientific observation of things themselves.

Insofar as he has pursued this opening that began in the nineteenth century, Geoffrey Jellicoe's work has developed accordingly with increasing rigour and persistence. In so doing, for most of his life he has inevitably found himself closer to some particular artists of his time than to landscape colleagues. Landscape had now increasingly to be recognised as the creation of the inner mind rather than of the eye itself.

The greatest single influence upon his work, correspondingly, has not been, as might first be thought, the Italian Renaissance garden, but the painting and writings of Paul Klee. The Thinking Eye[8] has become paramount, though the early influence of the Chinese masters of landscape painting Li-Ssu-Hsun and T'ung Ch'i-Ch'ang was also important. Like Alvar Aalto too, Jellicoe was influenced by the works of the Italian Renaissance of Giovanni Bellini (1450-1516), of Giorgione (1478-1510), and of Tintoretto (1518-94), or rather one should say by the landscape spaces within their paintings, in terms of spatial progression. The twentieth century concept of space-time reached Jellicoe, as it

8 *The Thinking Eye: The Notebooks of Paul Klee,* edited by Jüng Spiller, trans Ralph Mannheim, London, 1961.

reached many artists, in a growing awareness of cubism. But his familiarisation with the experiments of Paul Klee was categorically the most decisive influence.

The English landscape designer of the 1930s, Christopher Tunnard, had claimed in 1938 that what both the nineteenth and eighteenth century gardeners had in common was the desire to make pictures. He attempted himself, as Joseph Rykwert has pointed out, to create a space around buildings. But today 'the Park has atrophied'.[9] The idea of the Park has, for three hundred years, dominated English landscape design. As Niklaus Pevsner claimed: 'It was conceived by philosophers, writers, and virtuosi and not by architects and gardeners'. Gabriel Guevrekian's famous garden at Hyères in France, with its focal sculpture by Lipschitz, remained a picture under the blue sky, a figment no less of the picturesque.

For Jellicoe the Park has never been enough. Significantly, while careful to qualify his meaning, he has retained an admiration for the contribution of the civilised landscape to the English. The landscaped English country estate of the eighteenth century remains to his mind

> ...the greatest contribution we have made to the history of art. It was not merely an essay in the landscape sense, in the organisation of space; it symbolised a way of life that seemed to maintain a balance between the intellectual and the biological.

And there is a characteristic English rejection not of modernism but of the international style.

> There should be no such thing as an international style, such as was conceived in the 1930s, for the reduction of all design to a pattern would be to reduce us to the animal state.[10]

Within Jellicoe's work there runs a continuous identity with his roots, mediating the extremes of continental dogma. There lies perhaps a deeply held conviction that it is the landscape of his own land that surmounts any architectural pretensions. As Lionel Esher, another erstwhile colleague, of a younger generation, once put it: 'In the English landscape, the architectural elements are trees rather than buildings'.

Yet, since the birth of the picturesque, as Jellicoe has fully realised, the Park, no less than the estate, contains mythic allusions. The works of the eighteenth century English painter Richard Wilson are of that time, and seek to convey the idea of harmony, physical, natural and, therefore, social. As David Solkin, curator of a distinguished study of Wilson has indicated:

> Any serious attempt to comprehend Wilson's happy landscapes must take into account not only what they show but also what they leave out. What lies beneath those divisions or contrasts which are so overtly presented and so neatly reconciled? Understanding can begin only where the myth ends.[11]

Jellicoe has been conscious always of the underlying contradictions and tensions within cultures and societies. In his major *tours de force* he has, whether at Modena or Galveston, sought to separate seeming reality from truth. In the private

9 'Aesthetics and Technology' in the 'Garden of the Future', Joseph Rykwert, English trans (The Nature of Gardens), in *Rassegna,* 8 October, 1981, p5.
10 Jellicoe Papers, unpublished.
11 *Richard Wilson: The Landscape of Reaction,* David H Solkin, The Tate Gallery, 1982, p34.

Wilton House, Wiltshire, from the south-east, Richard Wilson, c 1758-60. The painting embodies the idea of the English Park with its physical, natural and social harmony. Courtesy Earl of Pembroke, Wilton House

projects, such as Shute or Asolo, he has reached perceptively into the world of the owner, to that inner self, the individual subconscious. On occasion, as at Hartwell, he has delved into the genius of the place in the absence of any tangible client, as a draughtsman might in Peter Greenaway's film, having a contract to fulfil regardless of prevailing circumstances.

The French philosopher Roland Barthes said of myth:

Myth hides nothing and flaunts nothing, it distorts. . . what the world supplies to myth is an historical reality, defined even if this goes back quite a while, by the way in which men have produced or used it: what myth gives back in return is a natural image of this reality.[12]

The problems posed by the traditions of the picturesque have much preoccupied artists in the late twentieth century. Both the American sculptors Richard Serra and Robert Smithson have been at great pains in their work to avoid 'the pictorial' approach.[13] Here background can be a highly prejudicial element. Unless the sculptor is aware of this influence, the ground plane simply becomes analogous to a picture plane. This is evident in Serra's 'Shift' (1970-2). Likewise Robert Smithson:

What most people know of Smithson's 'Spiral Jetty', for example is an image shot from a helicopter. When you actually see the work it has none of that purely graphic character. But if you reduce sculpture to the flat plane of the photograph you're denying the temporal experience of the work. You're not

12 *Mythologies*, R Barthes, trans A Lavers, New York, 1977, pp129, 142.
13 'A Picturesque Stroll Around Clara-Clara', Yve-Alain Bois, trans John Shepley, in *October: The First Decade, 1976-1986*, MIT Press, 1987, pp343-72.

'Shift', Richard Serra, 1970-2. Serra insisted that the spectator be aware of the deliberately indeterminate quality of the chosen site, a factor emphasised by the sculpture itself, in the abandonment of any suggestion of the picturesque idiom

only reducing the sculpture to a different scale for the purposes of consumption, but you're denying the real content of the work.[14]

In fact, Smithson solved his reservations about the picturesqueness resulting from aerial photography by substituting the cine-camera. The key was that by simulating the moving viewpoint of the observer, a greater reality and truth was evident.

Richard Serra took matters rather further, in rejecting the a priori techniques of the drawing board for on-site simulation and through full scaled mock-ups. This 'allows me to perceive structures I could not imagine'.

Yet all is not won. The way out of the dilemma is more complex. The theory of the picturesque applies now also to elevational or vertical treatment as much as it is generated by plans, as Serra seeks to demonstrate.

If the picturesque has to be displaced, there are fortunately already sound precedents in architectural history. Piranesi's concept of architectural space was founded on movement.[15] A particular *tour de force* he drew up for the benefit of his students deliberately exposed the demands of the baroque plan to ridicule. His 'Pianta di Ampio Magnifico Collegio' has as its sole purpose the provision of access to eight apparently useless stairways. Movement is structured on its own terms only: it has become the sole focus, a recycling process *ad infinitum*. In this way (and

14 Ibid.
15 *Opere Varie*, G-B Piranesi, 1750, pl 22: 'Pianta di Ampio Magnifico Collegio'.

this has been demonstrated at length elsewhere), Piranesi foreshadows the preoccupation of modern sculpture with 'passage', and that of modern architecture with 'promenade'; scarcely as such the lone discovery of Le Corbusier.

> This space, from Rodin to Serra, is one of passage and displacement from the centre, a space interrupted by the discontinuous time of involuntary memory, a slender space whose divergences it is up to the spectator to explore, while eventually connecting its threads for himself.[16]

Eisenstein, as a pioneer film maker, was particularly aware of this use of movement along a route as an end in itself, seemingly infinite in space.

The question arises as to what extent Geoffrey Jellicoe, through his affinity with and research into the sister arts of sculpture and painting, as distinct from the extension of a purely architectural sensibility, has succeeded far enough in breaking the hold of the picturesque tradition. From the evidence of the 1980s, it is apparent that as early as 1962 (at Cliveden, Buckinghamshire), the replacement of a classical layout by one derived from a painting by Paul Klee marked a new direction. In such a finite scheme, however, only a marker for the rejection of academicism can be effectively deduced.

16 *Passages in Modern Sculpture*, Rosalind Kraus, New York, 1977, pp280-7, gives fuller discussion of Serra's work and his concept of 'passage'..

'Spiral Jetty', Robert Smithson, 1970. Smithson would clearly wish to avoid being categorised as a picturesque artist, yet in using a helicopter to secure a representative view, he cannot, despite his endeavours, adequately distance himself or the viewer from the 'high image content' that denotes the picturesque tradition, itself here enhanced by an assumed local mythology

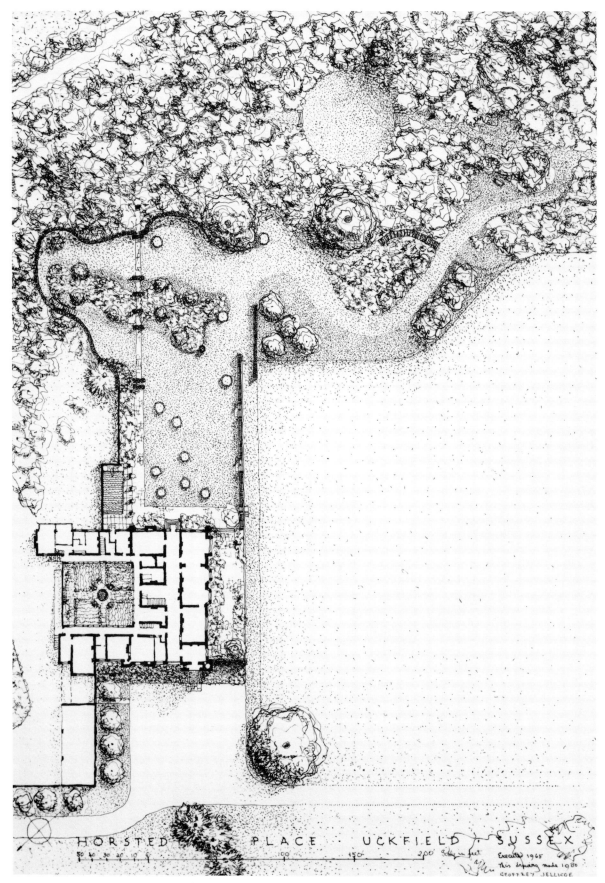

Site plan of Horsted Place drawn in 1980 by Jellicoe. The great woodland circle is top right

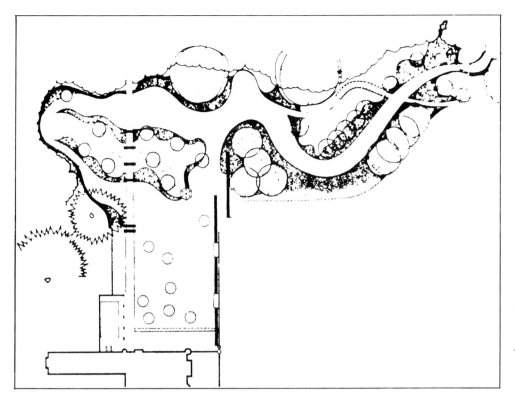

Replanting plan for Horsted Place, c 1965, describing movement as a flow of forces implied by planted elements, borders and edges, and paths. Drawn by F Tuson, 1965

The 1980s opened with Jellicoe's completed design for the gardens at Horsted Place, Sussex. Here 'flower baskets' (an idea derived from Repton) are positioned apparently randomly on a lawn and appear, both on plan and as viewed, as animate objects floating independently, as if on a green lake, across the lawn towards the woodlands and beyond.

Jellicoe designed Horsted in 1961, and sees it as a breakthrough in his development of the semblance of movement in landscape design. However, as he says:

> Some twenty-five years after the completion of Horsted I discussed the movement with the client, Lady Rupert Nevill (who had really inspired it). On comparing interpretations, I found that while I thought the movement of the baskets was away from the house towards the great woodland circle, the client had always imagined just the reverse — away from the circle towards the house.

Two elements in this design predominate and signify new developments in Jellicoe's design philosophy. Firstly, the idea of movement; and secondly the idea of waterscape.

At Horsted movement is simulated, of course, yet with a Proustian mood of reflective precision. There is accordingly an absolute rejection of the idea of the picture view, and indeed of the use of any directional axis. Indeed, the existing path is moved firmly 'off set' where it leads nowhere of significance. The path, in fact, is across the 'lake' (the lawn), which becomes a river entering the wood.

It has been commented that, in the case of the Moody Botanic Gardens designs, Jellicoe has provided everything but the twentieth century. At this point it is appropriate to point out that the twentieth century is diffused through the entire Moody scheme. The device adopted by Jellicoe for the movement of people through the complex series of set-pieces could only have been conceived in this way

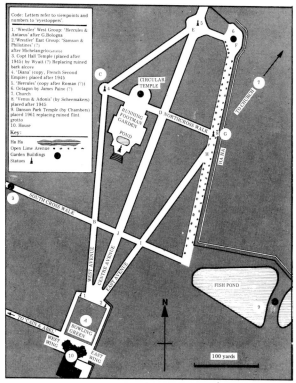

Code: Letters refer to viewpoints and numbers to 'eyestoppers'.

1. 'Wrestler' West Group: 'Hercules & Antaeus' after G.Bologna
2. 'Wrestler' East Group: 'Samson & Philistine' (?) after Michelangelo (attrib)
3. Copt Hall Temple (placed after 1945) by Wyatt (?) Replacing ruined bark alcove
4. 'Diana' (copy, French Second Empire) placed after 1945
5. 'Hercules' (copy after Roman (?))
6. Octagon by James Paine (?)
7. Church
8. 'Venus & Adonis' (by Scheemakers) placed after 1945
9. Danson Park Temple (by Chambers) placed 1961 replacing ruined flint grotto
10. House

Key:

Ha Ha
Open Lime Avenue
Garden Buildings
Statues

Diagram of the grounds of St Pauls, Walden Bury, Hertfordshire. Apart from the long walk on the right, all the main avenues refer back to the house — one of the many 'disillusionings' of the eye found in the grounds

The view from 'Diana' (placed after 1945) to 'Hercules' at The Bury, where 'images, fragments and content fall conveniently into a plausible whole'

St Pauls Walden Bury is a contrast of formal garden with elements of English picturesque. Here the dramatic rise of land in the central avenue gives that sense of movement which is one of the features of Jellicoe's garden designs

in the twentieth century. The water canal provides the route through a constantly changing scenario. The 'landscapes' are not so much pictures in the picturesque sense as 'montages'. And here Jellicoe exploits the discontinuities as much as the sequence allows. The last of the scenarios provided by Jellicoe (the caves at Lascaux) happens appropriately underground. The main canal passes through a kind of jetty stage; those visiting the caves must take a small boat running directly across this course on its subterranean purpose. The Moody drawings (pages 162, 163, 166, 167), completed in late 1988, demonstrate without compromise the degree to which Jellicoe has moved forward in the final decade.

If the garden at Shute was to be the essential laboratory for testing out such experiments, another place has, over a period of some fifty years, acted as a kind of experimental reference library for Geoffrey Jellicoe. St Paul's Walden Bury (The Bury), Hertfordshire, although derived from Le Nôtre, was actually laid out well beyond that period, around 1760/70.[17] It synthesises the formal structure of a Le Nôtre garden with elements of the eighteenth century English picturesque. But it is the creative tension between the two concepts, here coexisting in apparent harmony, which has for a half-century intrigued Jellicoe. The Bury interpolates wildness with formal beauty. The flower garden never intervenes in the landscape design. Furthermore, the plan gives no idea of the dramatic rise and descent that so characterises the central avenue. What Eisenstein referred to as 'the capacity of our eye to continue by inertia a movement once it has been given' is subtly and repeatedly disrupted by apparent distractions and disjunctions. At The Bury the topography and the unforeseen contours of the site are exploited to assist in this 'disillusioning' of the eye. The three avenues appear to be the same length, but the viewer comes to realise that this is illusory, and north of the North cross-walk, as a result of the disparity in lengths, images replace each other with unexpected suddenness. Right at the end of it all, images, fragments and content fall conveniently into a plausible whole again. In Richard Serra's terms, this is a work constructed in reality and in compliance with the natural order of the site: an aerial view would be as deceptive as any 'gestalt' representation.

Jellicoe's professional input here has been as occasional restorer/renovator. In 1978 he had reconstructed the original 'web' of avenues where in two cases it had suffered from nineteenth century degradations. The great avenue approach to the house from the east was to be 'restitched' in by new planting, and a restored focus of the avenue upon the octagon (which he himself had helped rebuild) at its climax restated. The family itself has largely maintained the original design in all other aspects. It is in this curatorship over a half-century and two generations of owners that Jellicoe has shared, to his advantage. On many an occasion, alone or with students, he has returned to this memory bank of landscape history, testing out the relative balance of picturesque and formalist meaning.

In the project for Modena, Geoffrey Jellicoe had already begun to dispense with the concept of the distinct urban park. He dealt with spatial disposition as fulfilling the psychological yearnings of the town dweller for space in parallax. In such a way Jellicoe reaches for a primordial configuration, not town park, not city adjunctive. In such yearnings, Jellicoe found that deeper psychological needs surface. Here he aligns with Bernard Tschumi (designer of the Parc de la Villette in Paris with whom Jellicoe had conferred at an important stage in its development) in seeking to define something which is less than categorical, yet which answers to current human needs in our environment for intellectual and spiritual freedom.[18] Such new worlds of the standard of Modena and Turin exist in contemporary projects. The difference is that the work is seldom entrusted to landscape architects by the architects who invariably control the principal brief. The importance of the solace of landscape is only gradually being recognised as of primary significance, over and above other elements in the built environment. It is the battle for recognition

17 'Blind Alleys and New Horizons: The Aesthetics of a Formal Garden', Simon Pugh, *Studio International,* vol 193, no 986, March/April 1987, pp90-8.
18 *Cinégramme Folie: Le Parc de la Villette,* Bernard Tschumi, Paris, 1987, and London, 1989. 'During the 20th century we have witnessed a shift in the concept of the park, which can no longer be separated from the concept of the city'. Tschumi claims that it is now necessary to oppose the notion of Olmsted, that 'in the park, the city is not supposed to exist. To create false hills hiding the periphérique ignores the power of urban reality'; see Chapter 1, 'An Urban Park for the 21st Century'.

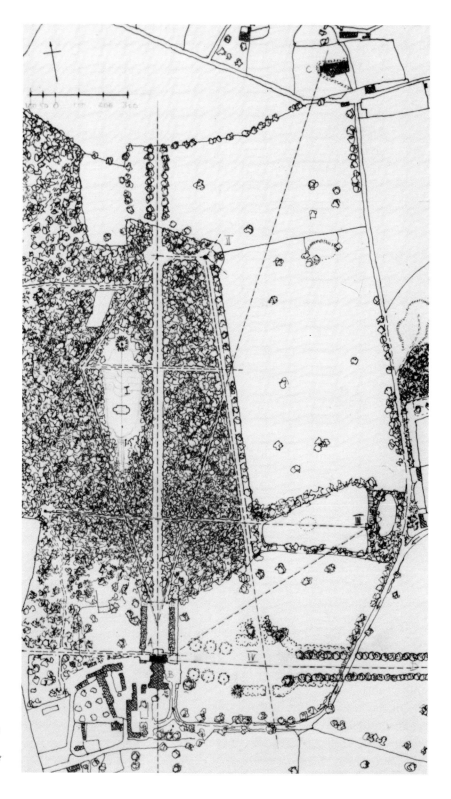

Plan of the grounds at St Pauls Walden Bury by Geoffrey Jellicoe, showing the reconstructed web area, marked IV. The avenue to the octagon which Jellicoe restored is the dotted line to the right of the figure IV running north and focused on the octagon

that Jellicoe has set himself to win. In the first instance it is won in the mind, and Jellicoe's route to the mind has been through the arts, especially through understanding the relationship of painting and thus landscape to the human mind.

One of the major elements of landscape design that Jellicoe has enlarged to play a key role in his work has been water in its various forms. It can be seen through the developing range of his work how he increasingly treats water as an element

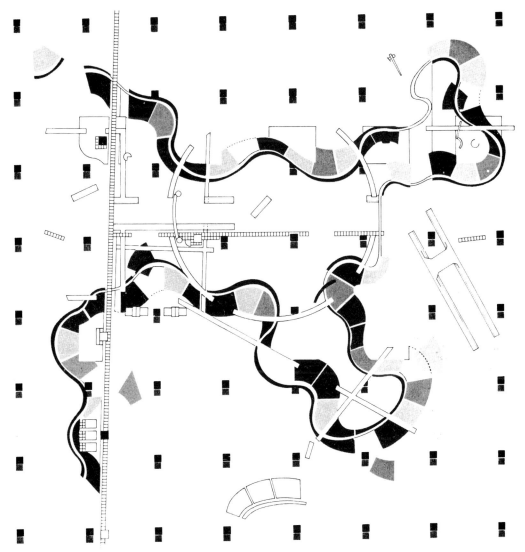

Jellicoe and Bernard Tschumi had discussed Tschumi's winning scheme for the development of the Parc de la Villette in Paris, in which the promenade of gardens was given a cinematic character. 'A montage of sequences and frames conceived as spaces for the interventions of artists, landscape designers, architects and philosophers. The promenade of gardens is designed as a film strip in which the soundtrack corresponds to the pedestrian path and the image track to the successive frames of specific gardens aimed at such activities as bathing, picnicking, rollerskating, as well as for displaying the staging of "natural" planting or conceptual gardens'

of movement and not as a static, purely reflective and passive force. His early experience of the Villa Gamberaia, its gardens and their eminent pools generated the semi-circular climax of the pool at Ditchley Park; latterly at Sutton Place, Modena, Brescia, and Galveston, water has become the essential definitive feature, without which these projects could not materialise as creative landscapes of any kind. At Ditchley it created the central axis; at Sutton Place it was celebrated on every side. For the latter he proposed, to the east, a sonorous cascade, contrasting on that side with the severity of the Nicholson white 'Marble Relief' reflected in the pool nearby; to the north, the way to the Moss Garden was made more evident by the necessary crossing of a recreated moat; to the west the great lake is viewed through the newly planted avenue of oaks; to the south lies a humorously laid out pool within a sheltering enclosure, itself containing an island for a table and chairs, from which to contemplate these enigmatic overlays.

If the Villa d'Este at Tivoli and the Villa Lante at Bagnaia were to Jellicoe the turning points that led him to become a landscape architect rather than purely a builder and gardener, it is clear that in both schemes water was a key design element that inspired him.

Writing in 1971, in his own publication *Water: the Use of Water in Landscape Architecture,* Jellicoe links water with architecture to create landscape design. And while admiring the water sculptures of Naum Gabo, and recognising the values of constructivism, in the same work he adds a cautionary note, prescient of the shift in values in the 1980s:

> If constructivism looks to the future for its life giving force, the arts arising from the biological sciences look to the past. Today the influence of the former (constructivism) is so predominant that a counter-movement seems to be taking place within us to redress the balance.[19]

Confronted with a project for a roof garden at Harvey's Store, Guildford, in the 1950s, Jellicoe produced a superb evocation of water landscape and sky, a secret archipelago of accessible nature, a world apart from the crowded streets of the town below. Conceived at the time of the first Russian space mission in the vessel Sputnik, it was a poem to the sky, made in water.

Water has been a primary element in Jellicoe's designs, and has enabled him to create his greatest achievements in garden and landscape design, but at least five other elements recur regularly in his work. The *Mound,* or elevated feature, is frequently created, if not already available to be emphasised by axis, route or vista. The *Fold,* or overlap giving textural break, is also not uncommon (as at Cheddar Gorge), as is the emphasis to *Edge,* whether static or moving in time, as at Hope, Derbyshire, or at Shute. *Vista* is sometimes pre-eminent, as with the lake at Sutton Place, but is more usually discounted, at least to secondary status; at Hartwell the vista is reversed, thrown back towards the house in an introspective game. And *Path* although, of course, in practical terms primary in terms of individual and collective movement on the site, is frequently pursued in an ambiguous manner, either through overlapping routes, repeat or reversal.

In the final analysis, as the various examples examined here in close detail seem to bear out, Jellicoe emerges as a manipulator of landscape form, as adept as his predecessors at deriving the greatest value from available raw materials on the ground. In dealing with his manifold clientele, an awareness of history and precedent has been used by Jellicoe to facilitate the education of his clients. This has seldom been any kind of barrier to the propagation of contemporary ideas as emerging from an unavowed modernist.

Historians may in future draw differing conclusions as to which projects constituted actual breakthroughs for Jellicoe. It is evident at this point that Cheddar Gorge in 1934, the Kennedy Memorial in 1964, and Sutton Place in 1980 were of major significance as key statements of the designer's principles. Shute was of a different more personal importance, as a source of experimentation with ready collaborators over a protracted period. Other projects, such as Stratford, the Rutherford Laboratory works at Harwell, and Modena, as public projects, served

19 *Water: The Use of Water in Landscape Architecture,* Geoffrey and Susan Jellicoe, London, 1971, pp32, 33.

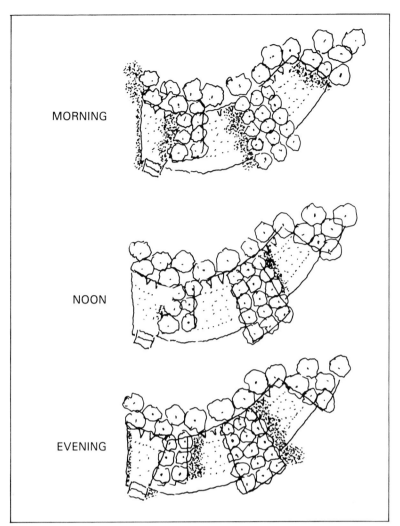

MORNING

NOON

EVENING

A series of contemplative gardens (1967), surrounding the site of the ancient cathedral of Armagh, with its ancient monastery and rebuilt cathedral, remind one of the elementary ordering of a sundial. The five enclosures enhance this concept, expressing the movement of the heavens; the first (top) is called morning, the third (centre) noon, and the fifth (bottom) evening. The times relate to the early Christian canonical hours of sext (9 am), terce (noon) and nones (3 pm) which Jellicoe found incised on a stone slab in neighbouring county Louth and, recalling the Celtic movement in design, Jellicoe sought to focus each of the first two gardens by plain grass-clad spaces; a third enclosure deals with nostalgia. The five gardens seem to change in nature as the sun moves. As Jellicoe says, it is we ourselves, however, who are in rotation. As at Runnymede, Jellicoe was here conscious of imponderables probing the subconscious. Such preoccupations were to develop apace for him in the following years

to develop Jellicoe's contemporary commitment to society.

Only in the lesser projects of the 1950s and 1960s, such as the Memorial Gardens proposal for Armagh or the Guildford roof garden, does the poetic fulfilment for which Jellicoe yearned break through against the welter of public projects that were the outcome of a busy professional practice — a time when he was heavily involved in the vital development of the fledgling landscape profession. The project from Stratford-on-Avon gives indications of Jellicoe's future priorities, but its execution is the victim of time pressures. Only in the 1980s, when he 'became' fully his own master, and when he had the isolation and the dedication to execute, laboriously but brilliantly, the great drawings, for Sutton Place, Modena, Galveston and latterly Turin, do the schemes do justice to his talents.

Well might the question again be asked, at the end of this century, 'Tell me,

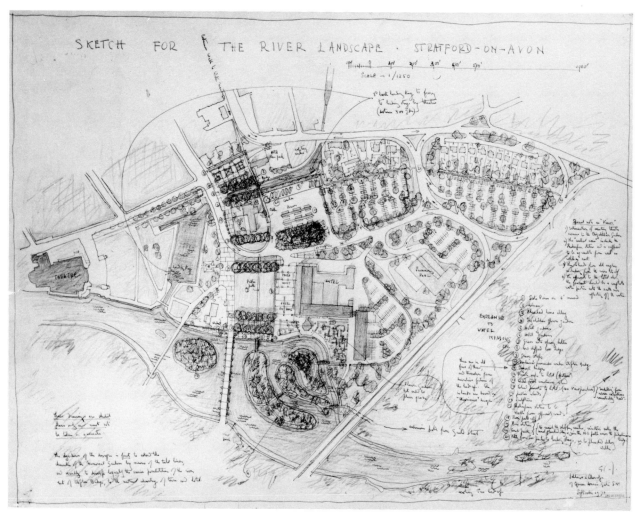

Sketch for the river landscape, Stratford-on-Avon, 1970. Jellicoe writes: 'This rough drawing was for office guidance only. It was sent by mistake to the planning authority, which unanimously gave it their blessing. I heard afterwards that the laymen thought it human. It was the beginning of all my future drawings.

'There was sentiment in the design. Forty years previously I had been concerned in a minor capacity with the architects of the Memorial Theatre, Scott, Chesterton and Shepherd (my partner-in-law). The gardens were now fully developed and my design was to expand the basic idea of the theatre and consume within its ethos hotel, existing public house and vast car parks. The plan has been realised except for the inability to connect the top of the hotel canal with the river proper — Midsummer Night's Island did not become a reality'

if anything was ever achieved?' For Jellicoe, the unexecuted projects remain. At least four of these may find he is no longer around to supervise, impossible as that may seem.

Ultimately, Geoffrey Jellicoe's success has been to return the art of landscape design to a pivotal position in environmental planning, as much a necessity to humanity as the provision of habitat itself. His understanding of the need of the human mind for an affinity with nature has helped remove landscape preoccupations away from the nineteenth century inheritance of the merely picturesque tradition and its romantic perforations. For Jellicoe, design has invariably required not simply vision, but intellectual capacity, and in his art both have always been present. If the legacy of the twentieth century in the field of landscape design has any value, it lies in the *oeuvre* of Geoffrey Jellicoe.

APPENDIX I
A CHRONOLOGY

1900	Born, Chelsea, London, 8 October
1902-5	Lived at Red House, Rustington, Sussex
1905-7	Lived at Willows, Rustington
1907	Preparatory School, Ruddy Roofs, Farnham Common
1910	School moved to Beaudesert Park, Henley-in-Arden
1913	Lived at The Vinery, Rustington, during school holidays
1915	Won Exhibition (Minor Scholarship) to Cheltenham College
1918	Left Cheltenham; determined to become an architect
1919	Met C F Voysey at Arts Club, Dover Street, London, who advised him to enrol as a student at Architectural Association School of Architecture, Bedford Square, London; enrolled at AA
1923-4	Rome Scholarship Finalist
	Travelled abroad with J C Shepherd to study Italian Renaissance gardens
1925	Publication of *The Italian Gardens of the Renaissance*
1926	Worked in London; joined office of Tubbs, Son & Duncan, Architects
	Set up in private practice as Shepherd & Jellicoe
	Designed garden for Sir Ernest Benn, Oxted, Surrey
1927	Publication of *Gardens and Design* (with J C Shepherd)
1929	Founder Member, Institute of Landscape Architects
1929-34	Studio Master, Architectural Association School, London
1931	With Elizabeth Scott and J C Shepherd won competition for Shakespeare Memorial Theatre, Stratford on Avon
	Established own practice at 40 Bloomsbury Square, London
1930	Bernard Webb Student, British School at Rome; six months European travel
1932	Publication of *Baroque Gardens of Austria*
1934-6	Cheddar George, Somerset
1936	Married Susan Pares, daughter of Sir Bernard Pares
	Settled in Grove Terrace, Highgate
1939-42	Principal, Architectural Association School of Architecture
1939-49	President, Institute of Landscape Architects
1954-68	Appointed Member of Royal Fine Art Commission
1954	Life President, International Federation of Landscape Architects
1960	Publication of *Studies in Landscape Design* vol 1; vol 2 (1966); vol 3 (1970)
1967-74	Trustee of the Tate Gallery, London
1963	Appointed CBE
1968	Publication of *Modern Private Gardens* (with Susan Jellicoe)
1971	Publication of *Water: The Uses of Water in Landscape Architecture* (with Susan Jellicoe)
1975	Publication of *The Landscape of Man* (with Susan Jellicoe)
1979	Knighted (Knight Bachelor)
1981	Recipient American Society of Landscape Architects Medal
1985	Sold Grove Terrace house; moved to Highpoint, Highgate
1986	Susan Jellicoe died
1989	Publication of *The Landscape of Civilisation: The Moody Historical Gardens*
1991	RA Elect

LANDSCAPE AND GARDEN DESIGNS
1929-1989

Work projected or executed by Geoffrey Jellicoe and considered by him to be significant

Broadway	1929-34
Cheddar Gorge	1934-6
Royal Lodge, Windsor	1936-9
Sandringham	1939 and 1947
Stanmore	1935
Ditchley Park	1935
The Holme	1936
St Pauls Walden Bury	1936-89
Newport	1941
Hope Cement Works	1942-88
Mablethorpe	1946
Hemel Hempsted	1947-59
Lusaka plan and hotel design	1947-52
Walsall Memorial Gardens	1949-52
Binghams Melcombe, Dorset	1949-79
Nottingham University	1955
Harvey's Roof Garden, Guildford	1956
Totnes, Devon	1957
Ruskin Drive, St Helens	1957
Guinness, Park Royal	1959
Harwell	1960
Oldbury Power Station	1960
Gloucester (Via Sacra)	1961
Cliveden, Buckinghamshire	1962
Crystal Span (Thames bridge)	1963
Christ Church Meadow, Oxford	1963
Kennedy Memorial, Runnymede	1964
Horsted, Sussex	1965
Isles of Scilly	1966
Grantham Crematorium	1966
Armagh Cathedral	1967
Isle of Sark	1967
Cheltenham	1968
Shute	1970-88
Stratford-on-Avon	1971-5
Chequers	1972
New Palace Yard, Westminster	1972-4
Exeter Cathedral steps	1974
Royal Horticultural Society, Wisley	1973
Tollcross Plan, Edinburgh	1973-4

Fitzroy Square, London	1972
Everton Park, Bedfordshire	1974
Baring estate, Hampshire	1975
Hartwell House, Buckinghamshire	1980
Sutton Place, Surrey	1980
Modena, Italy	1980
Brescia, Italy	1981
Moody Gardens, Galveston	1983-
Villa at Asolo, Italy	1988
Turin, Italy	1989-90

APPENDIX III
EXTRACT FROM 'GARDENS OF THE MOODY FOUNDATION'[1]

The Gardens are planned to open in the early 1990s, giving time for the further preparatory studies that are essential to make them the most scholarly as well as the most dramatic of their kind in garden history. The challenge is indeed breath-taking: to compress the experience of a time scale of four thousand years and the space scale of the globe into a time scale of a few hours and a space scale of 12 hectares. Clearly it cannot be done through realism; so it is being tried through surrealism as by the projection of the idea as the essence of a culture.

To the Reader

The voyage through time and space that you are about to undertake is not so topsy-turvy, nor as human and humorous as that of *Alice in Wonderland,* but the principle is the same. The world that you will experience is in three levels of unreality. The first is that you must regard the drawings much as Alice regarded the Looking Glass, as something to pass through to reach the world of imagination that lies beyond. The second unreality will be to enjoy sensuously those things that you must conjure up in your imagination, not only from what is shown on paper but all the multitude of unseen delights of eye and ear — trees, flowers, architecture, follies, sculpture, fountains, cascades, mountains, cliffs, grottoes and the changing yet unchanging waters that run like 'the thread of truth' (as the poet says) through all civilisation. The third unreality, that of a metaphysical experience, may not strike you until some time after your return.

Eden to England

We descend from the Campus, embark, pass between the wild savannah and the Giant Apple of Eden, and under the bridge to discover the spectacular vista of classical culture

1 Geoffrey Jellicoe, *Landscape Design,* journal of the Landscape Institute, No 172, April 1988, pp 18-22.

within their dividing water-walls; Egypt, Rome, Islam, the Middle Ages, 16th century Italy, 17th century France, 19th century England, and so to the dominating gods.

The Gods

As the water-bus passes the two gods peering over the wall from outer space and their spray is on our faces, let us pause a moment and, like them, ruminate on what is a turning point in the relation of man to his environment. Until this time the garden had expressed only one facet of the human mind — certainly by far the most important — that of the search for order and harmony in a hostile and often chaotic world. Under the placid surface of classicism, however, were rumblings emanating from the 'strange furnishings of the subconscious mind', so described by the historian Jacquetta Hawkes. These furnishings date from pre-history, beginning with forest and savannah and from time to time exploding into the civilised world. By 1700 the modern age, the age of reason, had been born and as a counter point to this had been born, too, the age of reasoned unreason; that is to say that the unknowns of the mind were to be idealised and translated into the environment.

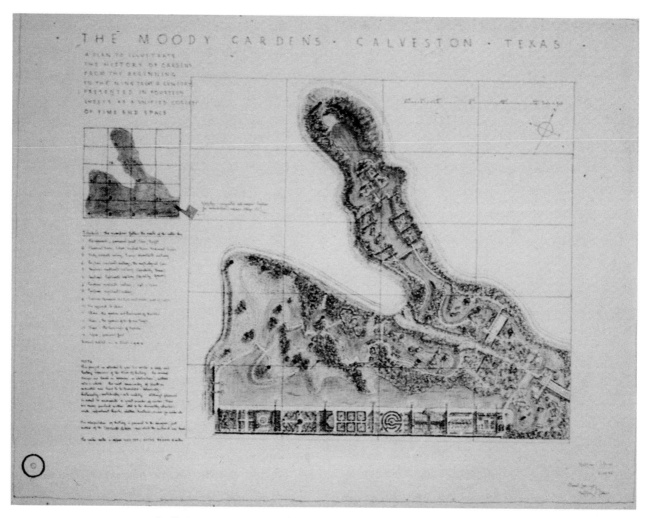

Geoffrey Jellicoe's drawing of the revised Moody Gardens scheme as described in the article 'Gardens of the Moody Foundation'. See also the illustrations on pages 162, 163, 166 and 167

188

A Revolution in Landscape

We progress through the everchanging landscapes of the second half of the European 18th century: the shades of Brown, Kent, Germany, France, Russia. The wall of the great mountain divide looms before us like some gigantic primeval monster. We plunge into darkness. We emerge from the darkness. The river is deeply set among cliffs and trees. The water seems to have changed. It has not. It is we who have changed; or should have changed.

[Subsequently the water-bus passes on to China and Japan.] Finally we are given a glimpse of a Zen Buddhist Garden of Contemplation...the greatest endeavours made by mortal man to bring infinity to this earth, and so through the primeval forest and through the looking glass to where we began.

INDEX

190

A CIVIC SPORTS PARK

Planned for the city of Turin, Italy and influenced by
the art of Pietro Mondrian, the design comprises a 'magic square'
for the individual as counterpoint to the landscape of the
collective (some 100,000 persons in all)

"Is it not possible to transfer and revive some of the vanishing
qualities of our historic city centres into the great modern parks now
being made on their perimeter?"

(Question asked at the Conference of the International Federation of Landscape
Architects, Boston, U.S.A, 16ᵗʰ July 1988)

The scale of the Plan

50   0   50   100 metres

250   0   250   500 metres
The scale of the Diagram

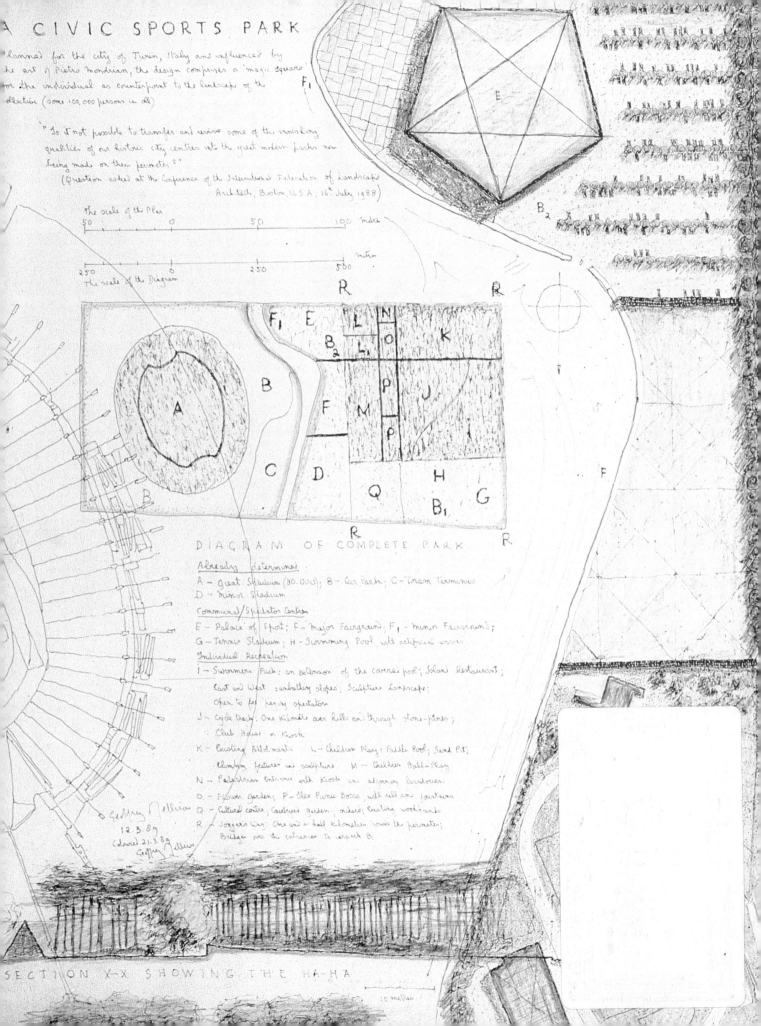

DIAGRAM OF COMPLETE PARK

Already determined
A – Great Stadium (80,000); B – Car Park; C – Tram Terminus
D – Minor Stadium

Communal/Spectator Centres
E – Palace of Sport; F – Major Fairground; F₁ – Minor Fairground;
G – Tennis Stadium; H – Swimming Pool with artificial waves

Individual Recreation
I – Swimmers Pool; an extension of the covered pool; Island Restaurant;
    East and West sunbathing slopes; Sculpture Landscape;
    Open to fee paying spectators

J – Cycle track; One kilometre over hills and through stone-pines;
    Club House or Kiosk

K – Existing Allotments   L – Children Play; Paddle Pool; Sand Pit;
    Climbing features and sculpture   M – Children Ball-Play

N – Pedestrian Entrance with Kiosk and adjoining lavatories.

O – Flower Garden; P – Ilex Picnic Bosco with rill and fountains

Q – Cultural centre; Courtyard Garden; arbors; Existing woodlands

R – Joggers Way; One and a half kilometres round the perimeter;
    Bridges over the entrances to carpark B.

Geoffrey Jellicoe
12.3.89
Coloured 21.3.89
Geoffrey Jellicoe

SECTION X-X SHOWING THE HA-HA

10 metres